Series Editor: Christina Jackson

Assistant Editor: Amanda Hopkins

Editorial Assistants: Felicitas Krause and Alice Taucher

Design: Dominique Michellod

Layout: Pierre Koechli

Vignettes: Max Thommen

Photography: cover and pp. 39, 40, 41 Vigo di Fassa Tourist Office; skier insert and pp. 24, 57, 66, 68, 98, 101, 129, 149, 151, 155 Jürg Donatsch; pp. 2–3, 19, 136, 137, 138, 139 Pinzolo Tourist Office; pp. 11, 12, 13, 22, 27, 31, 48, 49, 53, 54, 56, 59, 71, 73, 77, 80–81, 89, 106, 107, 110, 112, 116, 120, 122, 123, 125, 131, 133, 166, 171, 172, 175, 185, 186, 190, 192 Claude Huber; p. 17 Daniel Vittet; pp. 33, 37 Bormio Tourist Office; pp. 45, 46–47 Cervinia Tourist Office; pp. 64, 189 Corvara Tourist Office; pp. 84, 85, 86 Folgarida Tourist Office; pp. 91, 94 Livigno Tourist Office; p. 102 Madesimo Tourist Office; pp. 108, 114–115 Madonna di Campiglio Tourist Office; pp. 153, 154 Santa Cristina Tourist Office; pp. 162, 163, 164 San Vigilio Tourist Office; p. 170 Selva Gardena Tourist Office; pp. 176–177 Sestriere Tourist Office; pp. 181, 182–183 La Thuile Tourist Office.

Acknowledgments

We wish to thank all the local tourist offices for providing information, maps and photos, and ADAC Verlag GmbH, for allowing us access to the films of their piste maps. We are also grateful to Sally Brookes and David Gambia for their help in the preparation of this guide and to the Italian National Tourist Office in London and the Ski Club of Great Britain for assistance.

Cover photo: Vigo di Fassa; pp. 2–3 Pinzolo.

CONTENTS

Maps

Although we make every effort to ensure the accuracy of all the information in this book, changes occur incessantly. We cannot therefore take responsibility for facts, addresses and circumstances in general that are constantly subject to alteration.

All ratings of resorts in this guide were made without bias, partiality or prejudice and reflect the author's own subjective opinion. The information on the facts and figures pages was supplied by the resorts themselves. Prices shown are the most up to date available from the resort at the time of going to press. They should, however, only be taken as an indication of what to expect.

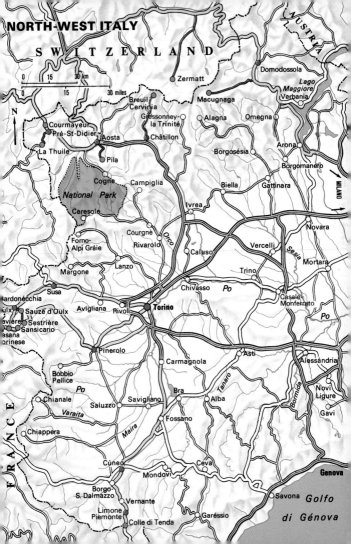

ITALY
AND ITS SKIING

Italy offers first-rate skiing—in a uniquely Italian way. Less intensity, perhaps, than its other Alpine neighbours, but more joie-de-vivre; less emphasis on performance, more on enjoyment. And along with the relaxed approach to life you'll find that inimitable style that Italians bring to everything from ski clothes to macaroni.

Internationally renowned resorts may be lacking, but a few names stand out: Courmayeur, Cortina d'Ampezzo, Cervinia combine exceptional skiing with an air of chic and elegance. Lesser-known villages, tucked away from the crowds (and in the past the taxman) up inaccessible mountain roads retain a more genuine Latin flavour. Few Italian resorts are purpose-built in the French sense. Most tend to be designed to look like non-purpose-built ones (e.g. La Villa), with rare exceptions such as Sansicario and Sestriere.

If Italy is not so immediately associated with skiing as, say, Austria or Switzerland, it should be remembered that it has in fact the lion's share of the Alps, with its own access to Mont Blanc (Monte Bianco: 4810 m.) and the Matterhorn (Monte Cervino: 4478 m.). The country's vast northern border stretches along the south-east of France, southern Switzerland and Austria, then north-west Yugoslavia, with ski resorts right the way along these borders.

The mountain scenery changes as you travel eastward from the towering white peaks of the French and Swiss Alps, to the precipices and pinky-grey pinnacles of the Brenta Dolomites (west of the Trento Valley) and the main Dolomites group to the east. The regions change too: Piedmont in the west includes the Aosta Valley resorts such as Courmayeur and La Thuile as well as the "Milky Way" resorts of Sauze d'Oulx, Sestriere, Sansicario and Italy's oldest ski resort—Claviere; Lombardy comprises Bormio, Santa Caterina, Livigno and half of the Passo Tonale; Trento takes in much of the Dolomites west and east, including

9

Madonna di Campiglio, the Val di Sole resorts of Folgarida and Marilleva, Monte Bondone and the other half of tiny Passo Tonale; Alto Adige in the centre of the Dolomite mountains contains Selva and the Val Gardena, the Fassa Valley and San Martino di Castrozza. Then in the north-eastern corner the Veneto, up above Venice, covers the eastern Dolomites, including Cortina d'Ampezzo.

Each region is divided into smaller ones, and you may find these sub-divisions particularly promoted in the Dolomites. Alta Badia, for example, takes in Corvara, Colfosco and La Villa. Centro Fassa contains Pozza and Vigo di Fassa and other smaller resorts. Each area has its own promotional logo and managing office in the major village. Resorts in these sectors are linked by piste or bus.

The Dolomites are one of Europe's most interesting skiing areas. Geologically unique, their structure was discovered in 1788 by French mineralogist Dieudonné Dolomieu, after whom the range was named. Jagged, straight-sided pinnacles tower high in the sky. The precipices are bare, exposing beautiful, ancient pinky-grey coloured rock which seems to glow in the morning and evening sun.

Another interesting feature of the Dolomites area is its recent political history. Much of the region is the South Tyrol, which was ceded to Italy at the end of World War I when the Austro-Hungarian empire collapsed. Whether the inhabitants were happy about this remains open to debate, but certainly attempts to Italianize the region in the past 70 years appear to have failed. Most towns and villages in the area have two names—for instance, among the ski resorts Selva is also Wolkenstein, Ortisei is also St. Ulrich. The architecture is distinctly Austrian, or rather Tyrolean—with wood and stone chalets. Most road signs are in German and Italian, and the local people speak both languages.

Recently, the revolutionary "Dolomiti Superski" lift pass was created. It covers nearly 500 lifts, 1,100 km. of piste and more than 25 resorts—all administered by a coded computer card that bleeps efficiently as you put it through an electronic reading machine at the bottom of each lift. Most impressive in areas like the Sella Ronda (Corvara, Colfosco, La Villa, Centro Fassa, Arabba), and Val Gardena (Selva, Ortisei, Santa Cristina) where it enables you to ski on and on from resort to resort with your "ski credit card" and be assured of lift access wherever you go.

This success story highlights the contradictions of Italian business sense: here a large number of resorts have got together; elsewhere the limited number of lifts in just one resort may be owned by different companies (or families). This sometimes means that lifts only 50 m. apart are not on the same lift pass, or that resorts linked by snow and lifts—such as those on the Milky Way—require a succession of passes in order to be skied.

There is a disadvantage for skiers in the Dolomites' structure, however. The mountains tend to have gentle lower slopes, suddenly developing into quasi precipices towards the summit. Much of the skiing, therefore, is on the gentle, low-lying areas with skiable passes between the fortress-like high peaks a rarity. The skiing around the Sella Ronda is not challenging for experts,

11

but that makes it all the more enjoyable for intermediates. Many advanced skiers, however, are happy to trundle around the easy slopes just for the experience of being able to ski without lift pass limitations.

If skiing hard all day is not your primary objective, Italy has many alternative pleasures to savour. Not least the food and wine, several leisurely courses of sheer culinary delight, whether on a sunny terrace at lunchtime or in a cheerful *trattoria* in the evening.

Italian cuisine needs no introduction—pizza and pasta in all its infinite variations have achieved popularity worldwide, but you can be sure that it will taste better here on its home ground. Despite the plethora of sauces for pasta, the essence of Italian

12

cooking is its simplicity: fish cooked with perhaps a touch of fennel, other seafood served straight, cold, as an hors d'oeuvre, Florentine steak charcoal-grilled, vegetables sautéed without elaborate disguise, at most marinated in lemon juice, olive oil and pepper.

Popular wines come from around Verona and Lake Garda, notably the velvety *Valpolicella* and the light *Bardolino*. Piedmont boasts some of Italy's finest reds, particularly the powerful, full-bodied *Barolo*. From south of Turin comes the sparkling *Asti Spumante*. The South Tyrol also has excellent local vintages, including *Riesling* and *Traminer* in the whites, *Lagrein-Kretzer* and *Santa Madalena* in the reds.

13

DOLOMITI SUPERSKI REGION

Whilst skiing in Italy, it's well worth taking a day off to take in some of Italy's cultural splendours that are accessible from the resorts. Turin, less than an hour away by rail from the Milky Way resorts, is best known for the giant Fiat automobile works, but the proud Piedmontese capital is far from being a dull or dismal factory town. The Ligurian coast, better known to holiday-makers as the Italian Riviera, is not a difficult day trip from the more southerly resorts. From the Val di Sole in the Brenta Dolomites there are numerous possibilities: Milan, Verona, Trento or Bolzano. This area is also near the Italian Lake District, with Como close at hand (though not really worth it in winter unless the weather is fine). Further north, in Lombardy, options include famous Swiss resorts such as St. Moritz, just over the border, or Bolzano again. From the Dolomites visit Innsbruck, Bolzano (the area's capital) and of course Venice—particularly accessible from eastern resorts such as Cortina d'Ampezzo (150 km. away), but only two or three hours from most of the Central Dolomite resorts.

If you don't fancy a full day away, the local town is always worth a visit—look out particularly for markets. Those keen on a bargain will have fun shopping around, and the prices for liquor are often much lower than the duty-free prices on the plane.

Wherever you eventually decide to go, it's unlikely that you won't enjoy a skiing holiday in Italy. Many of the resorts featured in this guide are genuinely unspoiled in a way that the more famous French, Swiss and Austrian resorts cannot claim to be. English may not be widely spoken, but non-Italian/German speakers can always get by thanks to the friendliness of the Italian mountain folk.

The common factor across the Italian mountains is a sense of real relaxation. In many of the villages, however, there is a feeling of a tourist boom bubbling under the surface. It must be hoped that the "Dolomiti Superski" pass points the way to the future for Italian skiing.

Familiar fare the world over, but at its best on its home ground, pizza is just one of the delights of Italian cuisine.

HOW THE RESORTS HAVE BEEN ASSESSED

Different skiers have different requirements, and their choice of resort is influenced by many factors. In addition to the resort descriptions and facts and figures sheets, we have assessed each resort in nine categories, rating each aspect according to a mark out of ten.

Skiing Conditions refers to the range of skiing on offer, the quality and efficiency of the lift installations, how accessible they are and how well they interlink, whether queues are a problem and whether the resort has access to the skiing areas of other resorts. If such is the case, the extent of the other resorts' skiing will also influence the mark that it obtains.

Snow Conditions are governed by the height of the resort (low ones will generally have poorer snow cover at either end of the season) and its top station, whether the slopes are north- or south-facing, and whether there are snow-making facilities. Due to climatic peculiarities, some low-lying resorts enjoy heavy snowfalls and a long season. Resorts with glacier skiing usually rate highly.

The three headings **For Beginners, For Intermediates** and **For Advanced Skiers** speak for themselves. Your standard of skiing should be a major consideration when selecting a resort, as nothing is more likely to guarantee a ruined holiday than finding yourself out of your depth if a less than expert skier or being obliged to trundle round easy slopes if you are looking for something to challenge your expertise. All resorts cater in some way for beginners; however, those that have attractive, snow-sure nursery slopes or a particularly good ski school will rate more highly.

Giving the full facts about children's facilities is especially difficult. A whole book could be written about skiing with children alone! The requirements of infant, five-, ten- or fifteen-year-old vary so enormously. Assuming that older children can be considered as adults in skiing terms, the **For Children** rating assesses a resort according to its facilities for the under-twelves, the provision of (or lack of) kindergartens both ski and non-ski, proximity and difficulty of lifts, whether there are discounts for children in ski school and on the lift pass, and if the resort is, in

general, a good place to take children. If a resort has special facilities for teenagers, it scores more highly.

For many, the **Après-Ski** is as important as the skiing. But for some, a night out can be as rewarding in a quiet hotel restaurant as in a raucous disco into the early hours. Nonetheless, the more lively the resort, the more it will score in this category, but you should also read the text carefully to be sure that the resort features the kind of après-ski you are looking for.

Non-skiers and the energetic also look to what else is on offer in a resort. **Other Sports** covers all the non-ski activities available, but also includes cross-country skiing.

Value for Money does not necessarily mean low prices. The criterion here is whether the goods or services are worth the price put upon them. Some resorts are notoriously overpriced: the cost of the lift pass does not reflect the skiing available or the hotels and bars charge excessively. Other resorts may have similar prices, but you get much more for your money.

A number of Berlitz **Skiers** (from one to five) has been attributed to each resort, in the same way as hotels are given star ratings. These represent the author's overall impression and are mainly based on how extensive the skiing and facilities are. You should look to the individual ratings and the general descriptions, however, in order to assess exactly how well suited the resort is to individual needs.

THE RESORTS AT A GLANCE

Resort	Altitude (metres)	Top Station (metres)	No. of Lifts	Runs (kilometres) *	Skier Rating	Skiing Conditions	Snow Conditions	For Beginners	For Intermediates	For Advanced Skiers	For Children	Après-Ski	Offer Sports	Value for Money
Aprica	1181	2309	29	55	3+	6	7	8	8	6	6	7	6	7
Arabba	1602	2950	26	45	3+	8	9	8	9	9	7	6	2	7
Bardonecchia	1312	2750	27	140	4	6	8	8	8	7	7	7	6	7
Bormio	1225	3012	24	85	4	8	7	7	8	7	8	8	8	8
Centro Fassa	1320	2213	26	45	3+	7	8	8	8	6	6	6	3	7
Cervinia	2050	3492	28	80	4	8	8	8	8	9	8	8	7	6
Cesana Torinese	1350	2300	5	300	2	3	6	5	5	6	5	5	1	5
Claviere	1760	2569	6	300	3+	8	8	4	7	8	3	6	2	7
Colfosco	1568	2550	53	150	4	8	8	7	9	8	6	7	8	7
Colle di Tenda	1400	2060	32	100	3+	8	8	8	8	7	8	4	2	7
Cortina d'Ampezzo	1224	3243	42	160	4+	8	9	7	9	8	7	9	8	7
Corvara	1645	2550	53	150	4	8	8	9	9	7	7	8	8	7
Courmayeur	1224	2756	35	95	4	8	9	8	8	8	8	8	3	8
Folgarida	1270	2179	13	150	3+	8	8	8	9	8	3	3	1	7
Foppolo	1600	2100	10	50	3	7	9	8	6	8	7	8	3	8
Livigno	1816	2800	28	85	4	8	9	8	5	6	8	7	2	8
Macugnaga	1327	2900	12	38	3+	8	9	8	9	9	7	7	2	8
Madesimo	1550	2884	21	50	3+	8	9	8	9	8	5	5	3	7

Madonna di Campiglio	1550	2500	31	150	4+	8	8	9	8	8	9	7	6
Marilleva	900	2179	11	150	4	8	7	9	8	6	4	4	6
Monte Bondone	984	2098	8	10	2+	7	8	4	2	6	4	2	7
Ortisei-St. Ulrich	1236	2518	6	175	3+	8	8	9	6	6	7	4	7
Passo Tonale	1883	3016	20	80	3+	9	8	7	5	6	7	5	7
Pejo	900	2400	7	15	3	6	7	7	6	6	4	5	5
Pila	1790	2620	12	70	3+	7	6	7	6	6	7	1	5
Pinzolo	800	2100	9	30	3+	8	8	8	7	7	7	1	8
San Martino di Castrozza	1450	2741	24	50	3+	8	8	8	8	7	7	5	7
Sansicario	1200	2700	13	300	3+	8	7	9	7	7	7	6	7
Santa Caterina	1738	2784	8	40	3+	8	8	8	8	7	7	6	7
Santa Cristina	1428	2498	17	175	4	8	7	9	5	7	6	3	7
San Vigilio	1201	2275	35	70	3+	9	9	8	6	7	8	2	7
Sauze d'Oulx	1509	2507	26	250	4	7	6	8	8	4	8	7	6
Selva-Wolkenstein	1563	2681	42	175	4	8	7	9	8	8	8	4	7
Sestriere	2035	2823	26	250	4	8	5	8	8	5	8	5	8
La Thuile	1450	2642	16	50	4	8	7	8	6	6	8	6	7
Trafoi	1600	2300	6	10	3+	9	8	6	3	7	7	7	7
La Villa	1433	2077	8	130	3	8	8	8	6	6	4	1	7

* with linked resorts

APRICA

Access: *Nearest airport:* Milan (2½ hrs.). *By road:* A22 motorway, exit Bolzano/Bozen, then via Edolo. *By rail:* to Tresenda or Edolo, then by bus.

Tourist Office: I-23031 Aprica. Tel. (0342) 74 61 13

Altitude: 1181 m. *Top:* 2309 m.	Ski areas: Baradello, Palabione, Magnolta/Belviso
Language: Italian	
Beds: 2,000 in hotels, 7,000 in apartments	Ski schools: Scuola Italiana di Sci Aprica, Scuola di Sci Full Ski Aprica
Population: 1,580	Linked resorts: None
Health: Doctor and fracture clinic in resort. *Hospital:* Edolo (15 km.)	Season: December to April
	Kindergarten: *Non-ski:* 2–14 years. *With ski:* 4–14 years
Runs: 55 km.	
Lifts: 29	

Prices: *Lift pass:* 6 days L. 110,000–125,000. *Ski school:* Group L. 65,000–75,000 for 6 half-days; private L. 23,000–25,000 per hour.

RATINGS

Skiing Conditions	Snow Conditions	For Beginners	For Intermediates	For Advanced Skiers	For Children	Après-Ski	Other Sports	Value for Money
6	7	8	8	6	6	7	6	7

THE RESORT

Aprica is situated in the Brenta Dolomites, to the west of the main Dolomites region. The village itself is a drawn-out affair, its wide main street reminiscent of an American frontier town, with a good selection of bars and shops along most of its 1500-m. length.

Though the resort is not as strongly Italian in design and feel as others, its clientele is still largely from its home country. A British presence is to be felt in the more lively nightspots, though, and quite a few Swiss and Germans hop over the border to enjoy the Italian good value. For skiers, the north-facing slopes normally mean good snow conditions, and there's snow-making on two of the nursery slopes.

THE SKIING

A somewhat scanty layout of lifts has left Aprica's 55 km. of runs spread out exclusively above the village on north-facing slopes. The vast majority are beginner to intermediate standard, carving medium-width trails down through the trees.

This is very much a beginner's resort, with no less than 15 short/medium-distance drag lifts rising parallel from the village. These areas are wide, gentle and catch the sun. Those wanting to test their prowess further can take the télécabine to a higher altitude and enjoy either beautiful long cruises (more than 10 km.) or a couple of rather easy reds and blacks, notably over on the popular Baradello slopes at the eastern end. Baradello and Magnolta (at the western extreme) sometimes require a lift-pass extension, even though they're on the same (not-too-well-linked) mountainside.

The highest point is Dosso Pasò (2600 m.). Advanced skiers won't find too much of a challenge, though one descent is classified World Cup standard. The Baradello and Magnolta sides claim black status for their one steep intermediate slope. Giant slalom races are held throughout the season and are open to the public.

APRÈS-SKI

There is a feeling of youthfulness and unsophisticated liveliness in the evening air of Aprica. The Charlie Brown discotheque is more popular with non-Italians, although the Boomerang advertises itself loudly by playing an interesting mix of music from an old van. There are plenty of bars and pâtisseries. The Pasticceria Corvi serves cocktails and pastries, as well as a burger, egg and chips special for those who can't survive the week on olive-oil-based food. There is a good cinema showing the latest Hollywood hits, though usually dubbed into Italian.

OTHER ACTIVITIES

A new sports complex includes an excellent Olympic-size indoor pool. There are two floodlit ice rinks and indoor tennis. You can even play American Pool in the Hotel Baitone Belviso bar. Cross-country skiing is possible at Pian di Gembro (6 km.) on the road to Trivigno.

Excursions are organized to Bormio, Livigno, St. Moritz and market day in nearby Edolo.

ARABBA

Access: *Nearest airport:* Venice (3 hrs.). *By road:* A22 motorway, exit Bressanone/Brixen, then via Brunico/Bruneck, Corvara. *By rail:* to Brunico/Bruneck or Belluno, then by bus.

Tourist Office: I-32020 Arabba. Tel. (0436) 79 13 0

Altitude: 1602 m. *Top:* 2950 m.	Ski areas: Porta Vescovo, Passo Pordoi, Monte Burz-Passo di Campolongo
Language: Italian	
Beds: 1,500	
Population: 350	Ski schools: Scuola di Sci di Arabba
Health: Doctor in Livinallongo (7 km.). *Hospital:* Agordo (44 km.).	Linked resorts: Ortisei, Campitello, Canazei, Colfosco, Corvara, San Cassiano, Santa Cristina, Selva, La Villa
Runs: 45 km.	
Lifts: 26	Season: December to April
	Kindergarten: None

Prices: *Lift pass:* 6 days L. 122,300–147,100 (children L. 85,900–103,000). *Ski school:* Group L. 25,000 per day; private L. 20,000 per hour.

RATINGS

Skiing Conditions	Snow Conditions	For Beginners	For Intermediates	For Advanced Skiers	For Children	Après-Ski	Other Sports	Value for Money
8	9	8	9	9	7	6	2	7

See also map p. 14–15.

THE RESORT

Between Selva to the west and Cortina to the east, Arabba lies in the central Dolomites. The village is rather quiet and suffers from limited sunlight in January and February; nonetheless, it is compact and from most accommodation you have only a short walk to the lifts. Furthermore, the skiing can safely be described as some of the best and most challenging in the Dolomites. The season is also one of the longest in the area.

The skiing is well matched by the scenery, which includes the Dolomites' centrepiece, the dramatic table-shaped Sella Massif. The colours of its rocks alone are stunning: even when the peaks are snow-covered, the spectacular pink and grey precipices glow magically in the sun.

THE SKIING

It is best to take advantage of the "Dolomiti Superski" pass covering nearly 500 interlinking lifts. For lifts to the Marmolada glacier (3342 m.), however, a daily supplement is levied.

North-facing slopes are reached by cable car or chair lift. This ski area, including Marmolada, is almost exclusive to Arabba, with only Malga Ciapela sharing the essentially red and black pistes. Snow bars, set up by enterprising locals, serve "ski in" drinks. The nursery slopes are south-facing. Chair lifts link into surrounding ski areas.

The Sella Ronda is a day-trip covering 60 km. and four mountain passes, which early intermediates could undertake.

APRÈS-SKI

Most bars, cafés and restaurants are attached to the hotels and pensions, so après-ski tends to be quiet. One of the most popular nightspots is the rustic bar attached to the Hotel Portavescovo. Late-night revelling is rather limited, but there is a discotheque in the Portavescovo.

OTHER ACTIVITIES

The natural ice rink is open four nights a week; on the other three evenings you can watch ice-hockey training. Heli-skiing is possible from neighbouring Corvara. The Hotel Portavescovo has table tennis, billiards and a card room. There is one short (8-km.) cross-country loop. A monthly market is held in the village, a weekly one in nearby Agordo.

BARDONECCHIA

Access: *Nearest airport:* Turin (2½ hrs.). *By road:* Fréjus Tunnel. *By rail:* station in resort.

Tourist Office: I-10052 Bardonecchia. Tel. (0122) 99 03 2

Altitude: 1312 m. *Top:* 2750 m.

Language: Italian

Beds: 1,350 in hotels and 350 in apartments

Population: 4,000

Health: Doctors and fracture clinic in resort. *Hospital:* Susa (37 km.)

Runs: 140 km.

Lifts: 27

Ski areas: Melezet, Campo Smith-Colomion, Jafferau, Les Arnauds

Ski schools: Scuola di Sci Bardonecchia, Scuola di Sci Fréjus 2000

Linked resorts: None

Season: Mid-December to end April; summer skiing

Kindergarten: *Non-ski:* from 1 year. *With ski:* from 3 years

Prices: *Lift pass:* 6 days L. 102,000–135,000. *Ski school:* Group L. 60,000–70,000 for 6 half-days; private L. 23,000 per hour.

RATINGS

Skiing Conditions	Snow Conditions	For Beginners	For Intermediates	For Advanced Skiers	For Children	Après-Ski	Other Sports	Value for Money
6	6	7	8	7	7	7	6	7

THE RESORT

One of Italy's oldest and most atmospheric resorts, Bardonecchia was frequented by the last Italian king, Umberto, and fascist dictator Mussolini. A town more than a pretty little village, its age ensures that there are plenty of interesting buildings, even if they're not neatly arranged in perfect picture postcard style.

THE SKIING

Although Bardonecchia offers a large number of well-maintained kilometres of piste, these are divided into two main areas, linked only by ski bus (included in your pass), so that skiing convenience is not brilliant. Piste gradings are not always clearly marked, so carry a map.

It's difficult to fault the range of skiing once you've reached the pistes, especially for intermediates. Monte Jafferau offers some excellent runs, including off-piste, above the thickly tree-covered lower slopes back to the valley station. The interconnecting Colomion and Melezet areas form the most extensive network, again particularly good for intermediates, but with several black runs, too.

During March and April, heli-skiing is available, and throughout the season the ski school offers monoski and ski ballet courses, off-piste ski courses, ski mountaineering (depending on snow conditions), parascending and a "Gran Galassia" tour to nearby resorts. There is summer skiing on the 3200-m. Sommeiller glacier, 25 km. by car from Bardonecchia.

APRÈS-SKI

Bardonecchia is noted for its reasonably priced restaurants, friendly locals and lively nightlife, especially at weekends when the population of Turin descends. Some of the more popular establishments include La Ciau bar/pizzeria and La Filanda pizzeria. The Ristorante Borgovecchio is famous for pasta. Late-night revellers will enjoy the Charlie Brown or Popeye discotheques. The town also has a cinema.

OTHER ACTIVITIES

The new Eurosport centre has indoor tennis, volleyball and basketball. There's a natural ice rink, and toboggans or ski bobs can be hired. There's also bowling and horse riding.

Cross-country skiers are well catered for, with 25 km. of tracks. There's a long cross-country link from Oulx to Valle Stretta, with an archery range en route to add a little variety.

The old town of Bardonecchia itself is worth a look round. The elegant central street, Via Medail, has a large selection of shops and interesting narrow side streets. The church should also be visited. Otherwise Chambéry is just through the tunnel, with the old town of Briançon even closer. Valfréjus, with which the resort may form ski links within the next few years, is another possibility. Being on a railway line (rare for Italian ski resorts) is a definite advantage.

BORMIO

Access: *Nearest airport:* Milan (5 hrs.). *By road:* N2 motorway to Lugano, then via Sondrio and Tirano. *By rail:* to Tirano, then by bus.

Tourist Office: I-23032 Bormio. Tel. (0342) 90 33 00

Altitude: 1225 m. *Top:* 3012 m.	Ski areas: San Colombano, Vallecetta
Language: Italian	
Beds: 3,161 in hotels, 3,000 in apartments	Ski schools: Scuola Nazionale di Sci Bormio, Scuola di Sci Anzi, Scuola di Sci Duemila, Scuola di Sci Capitani, Scuola di Sci Sertorelli
Population: 4,200	
Health: Doctors and fracture clinic in resort. *Hospital:* Sondalo (22 km.)	
	Linked resorts: None
Runs: 85 km.	Season: End November to May; summer skiing at Passo Stelvio
Lifts: 24	Kindergarten: None

Prices: *Lift pass:* 6 days L. 120,000 (children L. 105,000 for 7 days). *Ski school:* Group L. 70,000 for 6 half-days; private L. 27,000 per hour.

RATINGS

Skiing Conditions	Snow Conditions	For Beginners	For Intermediates	For Advanced Skiers	For Children	Après-Ski	Other Sports	Value for Money
8	8	8	8	7	7	8	8	8

THE RESORT

Bormio came to the fore in 1985 when it hosted the Alpine Ski World Championships, a fact that is likely to be maintained in its publicity material well into the next century. The practical manifestations left over for today's tourists are good sporting facilities and all the little extras that most Italian resorts lack—such as card telephones!

Bormio's importance as a key trading centre between Germany and Italy has been documented since the 12th century (nearby rock carvings date back much further). Situated in the Stelvio National Park, at the junction between three valleys, the resort is relatively compact, but loosely divided into old town—complete with cobbled roads—and new development. It's also a thermal spa town—the Roman Bath is still open, and there are mud baths and a new Olympic-size thermal swimming pool.

THE SKIING

The vast majority of Bormio's skiing is intermediate standard, on the north face of the Cima Bianca mountain (3012 m.). A dense network of lifts covers the slopes, two-thirds of which are equally densely tree-covered. It's possible to ski from top to bottom on either blue or red pistes—a 12½-km. descent, with a vertical drop of 1800 m. Beginners take the cable car to Bormio 2000 (a second cable car goes on to the top), where there are a number of snow-sure, gentle slopes. Advanced skiers should enjoy the 3-km. mogul-covered Stelvio pistes, created for the World Championships.

There is a second small skiing area over on Massucco (2205 m.), though just two drags serving one blue and one red run hardly justify the trip out of town.

Plenty of snow-making (thanks to the 1985 championships) helps cure an old problem of snow-shortage on the lower slopes—provided the temperatures are right (Bormio is not a particularly high resort). Summer skiing is possible on the Stelvio glacier (mid-May to October).

The lift pass also covers nearby Santa Caterina and not-so-near, duty-free Livigno (both linked by bus during the day). The ski school organizes heli-skiing, race training and ski touring.

APRÈS-SKI

Bormio has plenty of restaurants—notably the Taula, a converted 16th-century stable, or the renowned Baiona, outside town—as well as pizzerias, bars, discotheques and even a pub. The Palazzo Pentagono, opened for the 1985 championships, has a piano bar, film shows and arranges performances of folk groups.

OTHER ACTIVITIES

There's plenty of cross-country skiing (30 km.) in the valley, but this is often better up at Santa Caterina. There is an Olympic-size thermal swimming pool—with sauna (lovingly translated as "sweating grotto"), massage and Jacuzzi. The Palazzo del Ghiaccio houses a covered ice-rink, and there is also a natural rink.

Additional activities include tobogganing, tennis, and horse riding at nearby Val Zebru and in the Parco Nazionale dello Stelvio.

A wealth of material is on show for those interested in Bormio's past. The civic museum is open during shopping hours from Tuesday to Thursday, and briefly on other days. The civic library has similar opening hours, and those able to understand Latin/Italian may read of the trials of witches on the Bormio road in the 14th century. A second museum, open for a short period at weekends, recreates village life through the centuries, and there's also a geological museum and three churches, with stones and frescoes dating back to the 11th century.

There are a total of nine thermal springs in the area, already in use as far back as the 1st century A.D. Temperature ranges from 37 to 43°C.

Local buses run to Lake Como, Milan and Bolzano, and excursions are normally available to St. Moritz.

CENTRO FASSA

 +

Access: *Nearest airport:* Milan (3½ hrs.). *By road:* A22 motorway, exit Bolzano/Bozen. *By rail:* to Bolzano/Bozen or Trento, then by bus.

Tourist Office: I-38036 Pozza di Fassa. Tel. (0462) 64 11 7

Altitude: 1320 m. *Top:* 2213 m.

Language: Italian, Ladin

Beds: 5,059 in hotels, 3,528 in apartments

Population: 911

Health: Doctor in resort. *Hospital:* Cavalese (30 km.)

Runs: 45 km.

Lifts: 26

Ski areas: Buffaure, Ciampediè, Vidor, Alloch.

Ski schools: Scuola di Sci Vigo di Fassa-Passo Costalunga, Scuola di Sci Vajolet, Scuola di Sci Soraga-San Pellegrino.

Linked resorts: None

Season: December to April

Kindergarten: None

Prices: *Lift pass:* 6 days L. 147,100 (children L. 103,300). *Ski school:* Group L. 65,000 for 6 half-days; private L. 24,000 per hour.

RATINGS

Skiing Conditions	Snow Conditions	For Beginners	For Intermediates	For Advanced Skiers	For Children	Après-Ski	Other Sports	Value for Money
7	8	8	8	6	6	6	3	7

See also map p. 14–15.

THE RESORT

The Fassa Valley has been popular for more than a century with climbing enthusiasts and geologists. The first ski lifts were constructed in the early 1960s, with more comprehensive development in 1972/3. It is only in very recent years that winter tourism has matched that of the summer. With development continuing, most of the Fassa resorts have a feeling of newness about them—based on an ancient centre.

The two major villages are Pozza di Fassa and Vigo di Fassa (slightly larger). Both are reasonably compact at the centre, but continue to spread towards each other across a 2-km. divide. Next to Pozza is tiny Pera di Fassa. Below Vigo is the lowest resort in the area, Soraga at 1200 m. The spectacular pinnacles and precipices of the Western Dolomites tower above on both sides. The peaks are more erratic than the central Alps and, for many visitors, more stunning.

THE SKIING

A vast number of options are open to skiers in this rapidly developing area. All the resorts have their own skiing areas, and all are linked by a free ski bus (no lift pass required) which takes you on to Canazei and Campitello, both entry gates to the Sella Ronda circuit. From here, Val Gardena (Santa Cristina, Selva and Ortisei), or the Marmolada glacier (above Arabba) are accessible by ski. All these resorts (bar Marmolada) and many more are covered by the famous Dolomiti Superski lift pass. For the less adventurous a Fassa Valley pass covers most of the resorts on the initial bus route.

The Ciampediè area served by cable car from Vigo or Pera is an excellent beginner area. From Pozza, the Buffaure di Sopra plateau also offers good intermediate skiing on wide, open pistes, cutting down through the thick pine forests. Snow-making machines, capable of operating at -1°C and below (normally -6/7°C), ensure snow cover on these runs. There's also a higher

proportion of chair lifts and télécabines/cable cars than in many areas, and it's quite easy for the ascents of the day to be airborne only.

The wide areas served by snow-making machines, together with the computerized "bar-code" bleeping lift-pass readers, give the Fassa Valley, and indeed the whole Dolomite area, a feeling of high-tech development: here is holiday-skiing's future.

APRÈS-SKI

Restaurants, pizzerias and modern, comfortable bars abound, likewise on the pistes. Many of these are attached to large chalet-style hotels where the atmosphere is distinctly Austrian, but the prices tend towards the Italian (i.e. lower than in the Central Alps, though now often only marginally so). Fassa resorts can rarely be described as lively, but at the same time they are not dull. Perhaps "relaxed" is a suitable compromise. There is a cinema in Vigo.

OTHER ACTIVITIES

Traditional cross-country skiing is very popular here, with numerous short loops (graded red) and the famous Marcialonga 30-km. trail from Soraga to Canazei and back. On the last Sunday in January, this is the scene of a mass-entry fun race, attracting more than 6,000 participants.

42

There are large ice rinks (outdoor) in all of the villages; three bowling alleys; a swimming pool in Pozza; a pool, sauna and massage open to the public in the Hotel Gran Baita in Vigo; a billiards hall in Vigo; and more than 25 km. of prepared winter-walking trails in the valley. There is a museum of the local Ladin culture. Coach-excursion destinations include Cortina, Bolzano and Venice.

CERVINIA

Access: *Nearest airport:* Turin (2½ hrs.); Milan (3½ hrs.). *By road:* Grand St. Bernard Tunnel to Aosta, then via Châtillon. *By rail:* to Châtillon, then by bus.

Tourist Office: I-11021 Breuil-Cervinia. Tel. (0166) 94 91 36

Altitude: 2050 m. *Top:* 3492 m.	Ski areas: Plan Maison, Furggen, Plateau Rosà, Carosello
Language: Italian	Ski schools: Scuola di Sci del Cervino, Scuola di Sci Celoalto
Beds: 12,500	
Population: 720	Linked resorts: Zermatt (Switzerland), Valtournenche
Health: Doctors in Cervinia. *Hospital:* Aosta (52 km.)	Season: End November to mid-May
Runs: 80 km.	
Lifts: 28	Kindergarten: *Non-ski:* none. *With ski:* none, but ski school from 5 years

Prices: *Lift pass:* 6 days L. 130,000. *Ski school:* Group L. 90,000 for 6 half-days; private L. 20,000 per hour.

RATINGS

Skiing Conditions	Snow Conditions	For Beginners	For Intermediates	For Advanced Skiers	For Children	Après-Ski	Other Sports	Value for Money
8	9	5	9	9	5	8	7	6

THE RESORT

It is perhaps because of its three claims to fame—the longest piste in Europe, the highest piste in Europe (from Piccolo Cervino at nearly 3500 m.), and its position on the opposite side of the Matterhorn to Switzerland's jet-setting Zermatt—that Cervinia's failure to live up to its international status is so disappointing.

Ahead of its time 50 years ago when Mussolini changed its named from "Breuil" because it sounded too French (and boosted his ego by building, at the time, the world's longest and highest cable car there), the town is now a collection of ageing modern buildings. It survives on its obvious skiing potential (though with an increasingly inadequate and outdated lift organization), and its lively nightlife. The resort appears to have based its reputation and prices on Zermatt, without providing the charm or facilities. Even the most famous view of the Matterhorn isn't visible from the Italian side!

THE SKIING

Opportunities are vast, particularly compared to other Italian resorts. The snow and sun records are also exceptionally good, perhaps even marginally better than Zermatt in this instance. Wind, however, is a problem on the southern side of the Matterhorn, and outdated lifts are sometimes closed as a result.

One lift up from the village takes you to Plan Maison (2555 m.), which is the starting point for a number of gentle runs back down. The "real skiing", however, begins two successive parallel cable car rides further up to the Plateau Rosà (3480 m.), the main skiing area shared with Zermatt. Easy options are still available, but the Ventina run back to Cervinia is a little more adventurous. A left fork off the Ventina takes you down Europe's supposedly longest piste—22 km. of pleasant skiing all the way to the little village of Valtournenche.

If you don't fancy Plateau Rosà, another cable-car option takes you from Plan Maison to Furggen (3492 m.). At the top, you have to carry your skis down some 300 steps through a tunnel to the starting point of a black run back down to Plan Maison. Once you tire of cable cars, you'll find plenty of drag lifts, many of which radiate from Plan Maison.

The one alternative to the main mountainside is on Carosello (2480 m.), a small area of mainly red runs reached by a couple of chairs from the village.

Make sure you arm yourself one day with passport and Swiss francs for the trip over to Zermatt, best reached from Plateau Rosà. For the return trip, with a supplement to your regular pass, you can take the lift from Trockener Steg to the top of the Piccolo Cervino (know as the Klein Matterhorn on the Zermatt side). Here you walk through a cool tunnel cut through the tip of the mountain and then descend Europe's highest piste back to Italy. The air is certainly a bit thin. Regrettably, the mountain restaurants on the Italian side are famous for being inadequate, unhygienic and expensive.

APRÈS-SKI

"English pub serving draught beer" is listed as one of the après-ski facilities by several tour operators. Video bars (Yeti's), Italian ice-cream cafés (Dandalo's) and cocktail bars (Pippo's) all put in an appearance alongside numerous pizzerias. The Perroquet Bar and the Dragon Bar—which serves fast food and draught beer—are both popular with northern Europeans. There are very few establishments that could be described as top class, though the Café des Guides is a quite sophisticated restaurant. In any event, prices remain high, especially by Italian standards. Discotheques include La Chimera, B52 and the Etoile. It's very easy to have an excellent night out, especially if you finish off with a drink of *grolla*. This local speciality is served in wooden bowls and contains black coffee mixed with liqueurs, sugar and fruit.

OTHER ACTIVITIES

There are natural ice rinks (where hockey matches are played), motor bobs for hire and two 5-km. medium-graded cross-country

ski runs, plus bowling. One of the world's fastest natural bobsleigh runs (not open to the public) is at Lac Bleu to the east end of town, if you'd like to watch the experts. Swimming is a ten-minute bus ride away in Cieloalto or in the private Olympic-sized pool at the Hotel Cristallo. Helicopter rides are possible for those few with a lot of holiday spending money.

Left: Wrap up warm for some of Europe's highest skiing.
Right: A quiet moment on Cervinia's streets.

Strahlhorn
4190

Stockhorn
3405

Monte Rosa
4634

Breithorn
4165

Piccolo
Cervino
3883

Trockener Steg
2939

Schwarzsee
2583

Furgg
2432

Furggen
3492

Cime
Bianche
2911

Lago Goillet
2516

Plan Maison
2555

Edi

BREUIL-CERVINIA
2050

obba di Rollin
3899

Bettaforca

Valle di
Champoluc

Colle Sup.
Cime Bianche
2982

Roisetta
3321

Grand
Tournalin
3379

Colle Inf.
Cime Bianche
2826

Salette
2245

Cieloalto

VALTOURNENCHE

CESANA TORINESE

Access: *Nearest airport:* Turin (2½ hrs.). *By road:* Frèjus Tunnel, then via Oulx. *By rail:* to Oulx, then by bus.

Tourist Office: I-10054 Cesana. Tel. (0122) 89 20 2

Altitude: 1350 m. *Top:* 2300 m.	Lifts: 5 (Milky Way 100)
Language: Italian	Ski areas: Bercia, Sagna Longa
Beds: 610 in hotels, 4,500 in apartments	Ski schools: Scuola Italiana di Sci Sansicario-Cesana
Population: 400	Linked resorts: Claviere, Sansicario, Montgenèvre (France)
Health: Doctor in resort. *Hospital:* Briançon (18 km.)	Season: December to April
Runs: 34 km. with Claviere (Milky Way 300 km.)	Kindergarten: None

Prices: *Lift pass:* 6 days L. 130,000–140,000 (children L. 94,500). *Ski school:* L. 100,000–120,000 for 6 half-days; private L. 25,000 per hour.

RATINGS

Skiing Conditions	Snow Conditions	For Beginners	For Intermediates	For Advanced Skiers	For Children	Après-Ski	Other Sports	Value for Money
3	6	4	7	6	3	5	1	5

For map see p. 178–179.

THE RESORT

A small, traditional Italian mountain town on the valley floor between Sansicario and Claviere, Cesana is not especially ski oriented and hence has very little to offer skiers except lower prices than Sansicario. Due to its comparatively low altitude, there can be problems with the snow at either end of the season. For serious skiers this must be last choice on the "Milky Way" system.

THE SKIING

Cesana has little skiing of its own and combines its ski school with Sansicario up the valley. Two short chair lifts, beginning well above the village at La Combe, head off towards Sansicario in one direction and Claviere in the other. There are further chairs taking you up higher, or a baby lift at Pariol (1500 m.) on the Sansicario side, where the nursery slopes are.

Once you reach the skiing, though, the reds and blacks descending through the trees from the Monti della Luna ("Mountains of the Moon") on the Claviere side offer excellent skiing for advancing intermediates, with off-piste for experts. More cautious intermediates will enjoy a choice of reds above Sansicario, and an excursion, snow permitting, to Montgenèvre in France (take your passport just in case).

APRÈS-SKI

For those who enjoy a quiet village bar, served by quiet village folk, Cesana has a lot to offer. Those looking for lively, sophisticated or gastronomic experiences are set to be disappointed, despite the one discotheque.

OTHER ACTIVITIES

Cesana offers cross-country skiing and a floodlit toboggan run when the snow reaches the valley floor, where it tends to remain on sheltered north-facing slopes. There is also winter horse riding.

CLAVIERE

Access: *Nearest airport:* Turin (3 hrs.). *By road:* Fréjus Tunnel, then via Oulx. *By rail:* to Oulx, then by bus.

Tourist Office: I-10050 Claviere. Tel. (0122) 87 88 56

Altitude: 1760 m. *Top:* 2569 m.	Ski areas: Gimont, Pian del Sole, Bercia
Language: Italian, French	
Beds: 1,170	Ski schools: Scuola Italiana di Sci Claviere
Population: 180	Linked resorts: Cesana Torinese, Sansicario, Montgenèvre (France)
Health: Doctors in resort. *Hospital:* Susa (40 km.)	
Runs: 34 km. with Cesana (Milky Way 300 km.)	Season: November to April
	Kindergarten: None
Lifts: 6 (Milky Way 100)	

Prices: *Lift pass:* 6 days L. 110,000–130,000. *Ski school:* Group L. 80,000 for 6 half-days; private L. 25,000 per hour.

RATINGS

Skiing Conditions	Snow Conditions	For Beginners	For Intermediates	For Advanced Skiers	For Children	Après-Ski	Other Sports	Value for Money
8	8	7	9	8	6	6	2	7

For map see p. 178–179.

THE RESORT

Right on the border with France on the Milky Way (*Via Lattea*) circuit, Claviere makes its point by having a border post in the middle of the village. Despite this, Claviere is wholly Italian and claims to be the country's oldest ski resort. Despite—or perhaps because of—its frontier position, Claviere is an extremely relaxed little village made up of hotels, bars, relatively cheap alcohol shops and privately owned apartments. The whole is enclosed neatly in the surrounding woodland.

THE SKIING

If you want to exploit the whole of the Milky Way, Claviere is without doubt the best-placed serious ski resort to do it from. Local runs include two blacks, both with extra steep fall lines in places, on each side of the valley, plus enough good reds to fill a day or two's skiing. There are tricky nursery slopes next to the resort, others higher up the mountain.

Take your passport, and with one pass combination you can go through a ski-lift border point (easy to miss, though if you do so the guards tend to get angry). Once into France it's a black or red, a bit of trail-finding, a rickety old drag lift and you are at the top of Montgenèvre's ski-school test-piste.

In the other direction, there's access to a good range of skiing above Sansicario, via Cesana. With an extension pass and snow conditions on your side, you may even reach Sestriere and Sauze d'Oulx.

Lift passes cover either Claviere, Cesana and Montgenèvre *or* Claviere, Cesana and Sansicario. Rather than buy the expensive Milky Way pass, it's probably better to take the occasional daily extension, especially if snow conditions are anything less than perfect.

APRÈS-SKI

For a small, relaxed and personal village, Claviere's night-life can be lively. The "frontier town" feel and presence of border guards mean that the main street is rarely packed with merry revellers, but within the bars and discotheques a cosy atmosphere is ensured. There are two discotheques and about ten bars. There are no serious restaurants: most are attached to hotels.

OTHER ACTIVITIES

Cross-country skiing is popular, with a number of trails up and down the valley, including a loop to Montgenèvre and beyond. There's an outdoor natural ice rink, horse riding and tobogganing. Skidoos, monoskis and snow surf boards may be hired. Excursions are organized to Serre Chevalier and Grenoble in France, the Susa Valley and Turin.

COLFOSCO/ CORVARA

Access: : *Nearest airport:* Innsbruck (3 hrs.); Venice (4½ hrs.). *By road:* A22 motorway, exit Bressanone/Brixen, then via Brunico/ Bruneck. *By rail:* to Brunico/Bruneck, then by bus.

Tourist Office: I-39033 Corvara. Tel. (0471) 83 61 76
I-39030 Colfosco. Tel. (0471) 83 61 45

Altitude: 1645 m. (Corvara), 1568 m. (Colfosco) *Top:* 2550 m.	Ski areas: Boè, Campolongo, Pralongià, Col Alto, Passo Gardena
Language: Italian, German, Ladin	Ski schools: Scuola di Sci Corvara, Scuola di Sci Colfosco
Beds: 5,400	Linked resorts: Arabba, Campitello, Canazei, Ortisei, San Cassiano, Santa Cristina, Selva, La Villa
Population: 1,210	
Health: Doctor in resort. *Hospital:* Brunico (34 km.)	
Runs: 150 km. in Alta Badia	Season: December to 1 week after Easter
Lifts: 53 in Alta Badia	
	Kindergarten: *Non-ski:* from 3 years. *With ski:* from 3 years

Prices: *Lift pass:* 6 days L. 147,000 (children L. 103,000). *Ski school:* Group L. 14,500 for half-day; private L. 20,000 per hour.

RATINGS

Skiing Conditions	Snow Conditions	For Beginners	For Intermediates	For Advanced Skiers	For Children	Après-Ski	Other Sports	Value for Money
8	9	8	9	7	8	8	8	7

COLFOSCO – THE RESORT

Colfosco spreads for over a kilometre between Selva (Val Gardena) and neighbouring Corvara (2 km.), where the greater resort facilities and après-ski activities are situated. The two resorts promote themselves together as if the two were one. The link between them is by chair lift when skiing, so it is useful to have your own transport if you want to enjoy evening activities in the larger resort. There is no ski-bus link (though plenty of service buses every day), and the walk in winter is either along the main road or on cross-country trails. After the main, reasonably compact centre is left behind, the village spreads gently and sporadically uphill along the main road with large hotels every 100 m. or so over 2 km.

THE SKIING

Colfosco is part of the large Sella Ronda circuit that ski-links plenty of well-known resorts (including Arabba, Selva and Ortisei). High altitude normally ensures snow. Beginners will benefit from the resort's "exclusive skiing" (off the circuit's main route), which includes four or five pleasant but short, south-facing nursery slopes, three of which have snow-making facilities.

Corvara and the other Alta Badia resorts are easily reached via a horizontal chair-lift ride to the east along the Sella Ronda, or five successive drag lifts to the west, all the way to the ridge above Selva and down to Val Gardena. To the west, lifts rise to join the circuit served by the "Dolomiti Superski" pass. The runs back into Colfosco range from practically flat to easy-intermediate, access being their primary function.

Corvara to Arabba is an interesting day's expedition, or there is plenty of skiing from the large, nearly-flat, plateau above La Villa, San Cassiano and Corvara. This does contain one of the few downhills of note into La Villa, but you have to take a lot of drag lifts to get there and back.

The five drags (and a chair) up to the Val Gardena are more worthwhile for advancing intermediates. They're not as big a strain as they might sound, as they move relatively swiftly in a straight line, are well linked, and you do feel you're getting somewhere. Only as you near your goal does the piste map and actual marking become hazy. When this problem is overcome, the descents down to Selva from Danterceppies (2300 m.) are excellent long cruises, as good as the one from Piz La Villa down to La Villa itself, but with the added bonus of much better skiing to follow around the valley. The blue-graded 10-km. cruise back to Colfosco from Danterceppies at the end of the day alongside the drag lifts you came up makes it all seem even more worthwhile.

The computers on the lift turnstiles for all these resorts will bleep a merry welcome everywhere you care to ski. To think that the same is true right across the Dolomites almost gives a feeling of euphoria that such a feat is possible.

APRÈS-SKI

Bars and eating establishments are plentiful for a medium-sized resort. Garni Peter is a cramped but rustic bar, particularly popular with Germans and Austrians from early evening onwards, with a lively band frequently playing for tea dances and on into the small hours. The major hotel in the resort, the Cappella, just outside town, has live music and/or disco in the cellar and a good indoor swimming pool. Shopping in Colfosco is limited to newspapers, cans of drink, children's toys and salopettes from the general store.

OTHER ACTIVITIES

There is a small cross-country loop in Colfosco and another going on to Corvara. The top-class Hotel Kolfuschgerhof has a swimming pool and squash court. There's an ice rink with curling and ice hockey, while bowling, sauna, indoor tennis courts, parascending, snowsurf, monoski, telemark, skibob and heli-skiing are all available.

CORVARA – THE RESORT

Corvara is by far the largest village in the Alta Badia area, with more facilities than its neighbours. The wide main street has several little centres of activity along its length, and there is an army camp on the outskirts before the road leads into Colfosco, its sister resort. The architecture and atmosphere are typically Tyrolean.

THE SKIING

In the centre of the Sella Ronda, between Selva and the Val Gardena, La Villa and Arabba (all easily reached by ski and covered by the Dolomiti Superski pass), Corvara has two main ski areas, on the Alta Badia side to the east and the Boè side to the west.

The Alta Badia skiing is promoted along with neighbouring resorts La Villa and Colfosco, which share access. The mountain is not high (2140 m.) and the majority of runs are blue or green linked by numerous drags and chair lifts, for those who enjoy a gentle trundle around the slopes.

Above La Villa there are more challenging reds and a very good black descending from Piz La Villa (2077 m.). This drops 600 m. through the trees, with a hair-raising gradient. Across the road are steeper runs providing a more direct link with Arabba or leading to Colfosco and Selva.

If you take the horizontal chair lift to the west, you will reach neighbouring Colfosco, and from there five successive drag lifts and a chair take you to the Val Gardena. This is a minor expedition, but you can ski all the way back to Colfosco in under ten minutes if you're upper-intermediate standard.

It is possible to get to the Fassa Valley via the Sella Ronda and free ski bus. Although it's all on the same lift pass, you need to start out very early and be prepared to stop overnight or pay for a taxi if you run out of time.

APRÈS-SKI

Corvara is busy in comparison with other Sella Ronda resorts. There are nightclub/discotheques, plenty of sports facilities, and numerous bars and restaurants. One of the liveliest clubs from close-of-lifts is the Hotel Posta Zirm, where dancing continues all evening. The resort also has a cinema showing films usually in Italian or German.

A picturesque setting and access to extensive skiing make Corvara a first-class resort.

OTHER ACTIVITIES

There are a couple of small cross-country loops in the area and a 7-km. round trip to Colfosco.

The ice rink offers curling and ice hockey in addition to normal skating. Other activities include billiards, bowling, swimming in an indoor pool, squash, indoor tennis, paragliding, snowsurf, monoski, telemark, skibob and heli-skiing.

COLLE DI TENDA

Access: *Nearest airport:* Turin (2½ hrs.); Nice (2½ hrs.). *By road:* Grand St. Bernard Tunnel, then via Turin and Cuneo. *By rail:* to Limone Piemonte, then by bus.

Tourist Office: I-12015 Limone Piemonte. Tel. (0171) 92 10 1

Altitude: 1400 m. *Top:* 2060 m.	Lifts: 32
Language: Italian	Ski areas: Val di Cros, Sole
Beds: 350	Ski schools: Scuola di Sci Colle di Tenda
Population: 50	
Health: Doctor in resort. *Hospital:* Cuneo (25 km.)	Linked resorts: Limone Piemonte, Limonetto
Runs: 100 km. in Riserva Bianca	Season: December to April
	Kindergarten: None

Prices: *Lift pass:* 6 days L. 120,000. *Ski school:* Group L. 80,000 for half-day; private L. 25,000 per hour.

RATINGS

Skiing Conditions	Snow Conditions	For Beginners	For Intermediates	For Advanced Skiers	For Children	Après-Ski	Other Sports	Value for Money
8	8	7	8	7	7	4	2	7

THE RESORT

A collection of rectangular sandy-grey apartment blocks, pur-pose-built Colle di Tenda is in the Maritime Alps, above Monte Carlo, and right on the French-Italian border. The mountains here are less steep than in the high Alps, but this hasn't prevented a reasonably good ski range being developed.

THE SKIING

Colle di Tenda is in the midst of three valleys, with Limone Piemonte and Limonetto on either side. The whole area is known as the Riserva Bianca (White Reserve) and includes a ladies' World Cup downhill course. There is a good variety of pistes, including four blacks spread out across the three valleys on north-facing slopes.

At the start of the day you can either take a drag to the limited skiing area above Limonetto or the main chair up to Cima Pepino, above the main skiing area, which is shared with Limone. There

are plenty of blues and greens and reds here, as well as numerous, well-positioned drags up Bric Campanin. From Limone, a long chair rises to Capanna Chiara, serving a couple of equally long, good reds back. A further drag from there adds a bit of black to the top of your descent. The longest and best run, the Pista Olimpica descends from Monte Alpetta (2014 m.), turning red before it eventually reaches Limone.

One strange rule in Colle di Tenda is that residents in many of the resort's hotels and apartments are instructed to leave their equipment in a store by the bottom lifts, for which a charge is made. If your accommodation is well situated, you'll be able to ski back to it, conditions permitting.

APRÈS-SKI

Limited in scope, but inexpensive après-ski stretches to a couple of discotheques (one in the Hotel Fissore) and a few eating and drinking establishments. If you're going here on a package holiday, it's definitely best to opt for the organized evening events. Shopping is equally limited, though a bus will take you to neighbouring Limone Piemonte (or you can get there on skis), where there are more shops and a bank. Teenage children are best catered for here, with school parties filling a few of the discos and games rooms.

OTHER ACTIVITIES

There's a swimming pool in the Hotel Tre Amis, and toboggans for hire. For keen skaters with their own transport, there's a rink at Limonetto. Excursions to Monte Carlo can be arranged in groups.

CORTINA D'AMPEZZO

 +

Access: *Nearest airport:* Venice (3 hrs.). *By road:* A22 motorway, exit Bressanone/Brixen, then via Dobbiaco/Toblach. *By rail:* to Calalzo di Cadore or Dobbiaco/Toblach, then by bus.
Tourist Office: I-32043 Cortina d'Ampezzo. Tel. (0436) 32 31

Altitude: 1224 m. *Top:* 3243 m.	Lifts: 42
Language: Italian	Ski areas: Falzarego, Tofana, Cristallo, Faloria
Beds: 4,500 in hotels, 18,000 in apartments and *pensioni*	
	Ski schools: Scuola di Sci Cortina, Scuola di Sci Azzurra Cortina
Population: 7,700	
Health: Doctors, dentists and fracture clinic in resort. *Hospital:* Pieve di Cadore or San Candido (30 km.)	Linked resorts: None
	Season: December to April
	Kindergarten: None
Runs: 160 km.	

Prices: *Lift pass:* 6 days L. 125,400–150,000 (children L. 100,000). *Ski school:* Group L. 115,000-130,000 for 6 half-days (reduction for children under 15); private L. 32,000 per hour.

RATINGS

Skiing Conditions	Snow Conditions	For Beginners	For Intermediates	For Advanced Skiers	For Children	Après-Ski	Other Sports	Value for Money
8	8	9	9	8	7	9	8	7

See also map p. 14–15.

THE RESORT

Ranking alongside Swiss Wengen and Mürren for history and St. Moritz for style, Cortina is one of the grand old breed of ski resorts, famous for more than half a century and for all the right reasons. A wide variety of skiing is matched by a vast selection of alternatives. It is a resort with all the facilities required for a well-rounded holiday. As it is traditionally home of the chic, ski-scruffs will still feel out of place in Cortina, where ski prowess is definitely not the be all and end all. The resort was the Olympic host in 1956.

THE SKIING

Italy's most famous ski resort lies at the eastern extremity of the Dolomiti Superski pass area which offers the benefits of over a thousand kilometres of piste (albeit not linked by lifts). In any case Cortina has plenty of skiing of its own, in spectacular mountain scenery. Traditional though Cortina may be, the beloved "bleep" of the high-tech computer pass control, for which Dolomiti Superski resorts are famous, echoes around the intricate network of pistes.

Beginners have a choice of nursery slopes in the Pierosà, Mietres and Socrepes areas. Much of Cortina's (and indeed the Dolomites') skiing appears to have been designed for intermediates. An excellent 10-km. piste runs from Lagazuoi over the first mountains towards San Cassiano. Advanced skiers should be impressed by the statistics: a 2000-m. vertical drop from the top station to the village. Two of the best descents are from Tofana (start of the Olympic men's downhill). The Staunies provides several menacing blacks.

APRÈS-SKI

Though you may have your doubts about how genuine the atmosphere is (with the excess of fur coats), there can be no denying that Cortina is a lively place with an awful lot going on. There are simply too many bars and restaurants to make it fair to single any out. One exception might be the new Hong Kong Chinese restaurant. Nightclubs abound and possibilities for dancing to live music are endless. What you will need is money: drinks prices can be exorbitant, but if you shop around, it is possible to avoid breaking the bank.

OTHER ACTIVITIES

Facilities for cross-country skiers are virtually incomparable. They include a recently opened, well-marked trail stretching no less than 210 km. crossing the regions of Veneto, Alto Adige, East Tyrol and Carinthia before arriving in Villach in Austria. The route can be completed in six stages and there is an arrangement for luggage to be forwarded to participating hotels. In addition, there are 74 local cross-country trails.

The resort has many cultural and "extra-curricular" activities organized throughout the year. January is a particularly busy month, with a veteran car race, a horse race on snow and a dog sled race—all attracting international competition.

Also on offer is an Olympic ice rink (with ice disco on occasions), Olympic ski jump, bobsleigh run and ice hockey. The Hotel Miramonti has an indoor swimming pool open to non-residents, and many hotels have their own sauna and solarium. There are covered tennis courts and a bowling alley. Most alternative snow sports are available, as well as pony trekking and snow-shoe walking.

The "Cortina Card" (available in the resort) gives visitors discounted access to most sporting facilities, savings in many other establishments and on services.

There's a local history museum, art gallery and civic library, and for further diversion you can take a trip down to Venice.

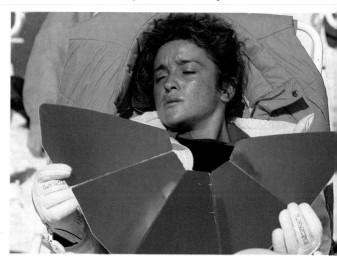

COURMAYEUR

Access: *Nearest airport:* Geneva (2 hrs.); Turin (3 hrs.). *By road:* A40 motorway, then via Chamonix and Mont Blanc Tunnel. *By rail:* to Pré-St-Didier, then by bus.

Tourist Office: I-11013 Courmayeur. Tel. (0165) 84 20 60

Altitude: 1224 m. *Top:* 2756 m.	Ski areas: Chécrouit-Val Veny, Col du Géant
Language: Italian	
Beds: 2,700 in hotels, 13,800 in apartments and chalets	Ski schools: Scuola di Sci del Monte Bianco
Population: 2,765	Linked resorts: None
Health: Doctor and fracture clinic in resort. *Hospital:* Aosta (37 km.)	Season: December to April; summer skiing
Runs: 95 km.	Kindergarten: *Non-ski:* none. *With ski:* 5–10 years
Lifts: 35	

Prices: *Lift pass:* 6 days L. 129,000-152,000. *Ski school:* Group L. 96,000 for 6 half-days; private L. 22,000 per hour.

RATINGS

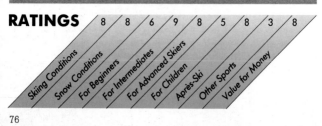

Skiing Conditions	Snow Conditions	For Beginners	For Intermediates	For Advanced Skiers	For Children	Après-Ski	Other Sports	Value for Money
8	8	6	9	8	5	8	3	8

THE RESORT

Undoubtedly one of Italy's most popular skiing destinations, Courmayeur wins on its traditional village atmosphere, welcoming residents and easy accessibility (just beyond the Mont Blanc tunnel). It's this combination that's led the resort to be labelled by numerous contented visitors as possibly the happiest and friendliest resort in the Alps. All it has lost during its 50-odd years of popularity is the duty-free status it once had. Situated as it is in the historic Aosta Valley, the surrounding views of the Mont Blanc range are particularly spectacular.

THE SKIING

It's normally a bit of a walk to the lifts and back again, as skiing down to most areas of the village is not possible. But once you're up, it's glorious, not least because of the 24 mountain restaurants and bars from which to choose.

It all begins at Plan Chécrouit, a rather uncomfortable cable-car ride up, where the nursery slopes (and first restaurants) are. From here the resort's skiing opens up, with numerous, mainly intermediate runs a further lift ride or two away. An exciting adventure for advanced skiers is the 10 km. from Cresta d'Arp to Dolonne, with a vertical drop of 1500 m. Off-piste is extensive.

78

The three-stage cable car from La Palud (just out of town) takes you to one of the most beautiful runs, a spectacular off-piste descent of 18 km. down from Punta Helbronner along the Vallée Blanche to French Chamonix, from where you take the bus back. The action-packed descent back on the Italian side over the Toula glacier should not be undertaken without a guide.

There are some good nursery slopes, and the ski school is popular, but this is not really a recommended beginners' resort.

The lift pass covers the Mont Blanc area for one day a week. There's also a once-weekly lift pass swap, when those in Courmayeur can ski for a day in Cervinia, and vice versa. But, although the Aosta Valley (of which Courmayeur, Cervinia, La Thuile, Pila and others are parts) is promoting itself collectively, lift passes are still limited to individual resorts.

APRÈS-SKI

The main street, Via Roma, is the après-ski centre. The American Bar and neighbouring Caffè della Posta are friendly rivals, with the former offering interesting cocktails, the latter content to serve various great, traditional and sometimes unique beverages. For "real English beer on draught", the Leone Rosso is opposite.

Numerous restaurants with high standards and fairly reasonable prices make a bed and breakfast accommodation package very worthwhile. Absolutely everyone goes to the Maison de Filippo restaurant at nearby Entrèves. There are also two cinemas.

OTHER ACTIVITIES

With 22 km. of prepared tracks, cross-country facilities are good, and there are regular buses (15 minutes) to the Val Ferret area where it's based. Indoor and outdoor pools can be found at two hotels, but these are not often open to the public. There are sauna facilities and an artificial ice rink (with ice discotheque).

The Wednesday street market should not be missed, but there's a good selection of shops in any case. If you have a few free hours, visit the fascinating museum of local culture and history.

FOLGARIDA

 +

Access: *Nearest airport:* Verona (2½ hrs.); Innsbruck (2½ hrs.).
By road: A22 motorway, exit San Michele, then via Dimaro. *By rail:* to Trento, then private line to Malè and bus.

Tourist Office: I-38025 Folgarida. Tel. (0463) 96 11 3

Altitude: 1270 m. *Top:* 2179 m.	Ski areas: Monte Vigo, Monte Spolverino, Belvedere, Malghet Haut
Language: Italian	
Beds: 1,600 in hotels, 1,000 in apartments	Ski schools: Scuola Italiana di Sci Dimaro-Folgarida
Population: 64	Linked resorts: Marilleva, Madonna di Campiglio
Health: Doctor in resort. *Hospital:* Cles (27 km.)	Season: Christmas to Easter
Runs: 40 km. (150 km. for whole area)	Kindergarten: None
Lifts: 13	

Prices: *Lift pass:* 7 days Folgarida-Marilleva L. 125,000–140,000 (children L. 105,000–110,000). *Ski school:* Group L. 60,000–65,000 for 6 half-days; private L. 30,000 per hour.

RATINGS

Skiing Conditions	Snow Conditions	For Beginners	For Intermediates	For Advanced Skiers	For Children	Après-Ski	Other Sports	Value for Money
8	8	8	9	8	7	3	1	7

See also map p. 127.

THE RESORT

Small, usually quiet, and really quite pleasant by purpose-built standards, Folgarida is well placed in the northern Brenta Dolomites, west of the main group, and is reached via an especially winding mountain road. Surrounded by thickly wooded slopes, the village is ideally situated for access to the 150-km. of varied piste linking close neighbours Marilleva and Madonna di Campiglio over the mountain.

THE SKIING

More than half of Folgarida's own skiing consists of green and blue runs on north-east-facing slopes, so there's plenty for beginners and intermediates. A cable car rises from the village to Malghet Haut at 1850 m. which is also the arrival point of the resort's other access lift, a chair. From here another short chair rises to two even shorter drag lifts, mainly of service to the ski school, or a longer chair goes up to Spolverino (2092 m.) where a blue takes you to the base of the Monte Vigo lift.

Monte Vigo (2179 m.) is the highest point and roundabout for traffic heading to the other resorts on this circuit. From here you can take a short not-too-difficult red and a further chair over to Madonna di Campiglio due south, or head north to Marilleva down either long straight blues or steep blacks.

Alternatively, you might take a trip down Folgarida's only south-east-facing slope, a red, which gives you the option of either returning to the middle station (and on to the resort), or reaching a dead end and taking the chair back up to Spolverino.

There is a single black, the "Nera Folgarida", often mogulled, running beneath the télécabine back to the village. This makes a good end to the day for advanced skiers returning from Madonna di Campiglio's more challenging slopes.

Since the main skiing starts at a reasonable altitude, snow cover is rarely a problem. In any case more than 6 km. of the lower slopes benefit from snow-making machines.

APRÈS-SKI

This is mainly a do-it-yourself resort for the professional après-skier. Bars and restaurants are part of the hotels. Tour operators will have their own range of organized evening activities; otherwise there are three discotheques.

OTHER ACTIVITIES

This is not a great base for cross-country skiers, with the nearest trails starting 6 km. away. The whole area commands spectacular views of the Val di Sole and of the Dolomites craggy peaks from the top.

FOPPOLO

Access: *Nearest airport:* Milan (2 hrs.). *By road:* A4 motorway, exit Dalmine, then via San Pellegrino. *By rail:* to Bergamo, then by bus.

Tourist Office: I-24010 Foppolo. Tel. (0345) 74 17 5

Altitude: 1600 m. *Top:* 2100 m.	Lifts: 10
Language: Italian	Ski areas: Valgussera-Monte-bello-Foppane, Carisole, Monte Toro
Beds: 400 in hotels, 2,000 in apartments	
Population: 200	Ski schools: Scuola Italiana di Sci Foppolo
Health: Doctors and fracture clinic in resort. *Hospital:* San Giovanni Bianco (28 km.)	Linked resorts: Carona
	Season: December to May
Runs: 50 km.	Kindergarten: None

Prices: *Lift pass:* 6 days L. 80,000–105,000. *Ski school:* Group L. 70,000 for 6 half-days; private L. 25,000 per hour.

RATINGS

Skiing Conditions	Snow Conditions	For Beginners	For Intermediates	For Advanced Skiers	For Children	Après-Ski	Other Sports	Value for Money
7	8	9	6	2	7	7	3	8

THE RESORT

Foppolo lies at a good altitude at the head of the Brembana Valley, with no busy through roads to cross in ski boots with skis over your shoulder. It's the common Italian tale of little village cashing in on the ski boom. Built on a steep hillside, the old centre is on a lower level than the newer tourist area. It boasts a very attractive little church, one of several along the valley road. For its size, Foppolo is a well-equipped village and has attracted more than average interest from British and other foreign tour operators.

THE SKIING

Essentially a beginner/early-intermediate resort, Foppolo's altitude usually ensures that the village-side nursery slopes have the snow cover that similar planning in other resorts often fails to achieve.

The majority of the pistes fan out north-eastward, served by chair or drag lift. One chair takes you up to Valgussera (2200 m.), which leads to the Giretta area or to Quarta Baita (1820 m.), also reached by chair and a drag from the village. From here more lifts rise to Montebello (2100 m.), where there is a restaurant.

The run from Quarta Baita back to Foppolo is absolutely superb for beginners, the gentle but long chair (turned off when not in use during the low season, but on again as soon as someone wishes to ascend) eradicates the usual early drag-lift problems.

From Giretta there are a further four lifts to be found. These are above the neighbouring village of Carona (1100 m.), so be careful to check that your lift pass covers them. Though the pistes of both resorts come within 50 m. of each other, there is, amazingly enough, no marked link, a great problem in fog or poor conditions.

To the north of the village two drags go to Foppane, where a choice of red or blue runs leads back to the resort.

The skiing is certainly enjoyable for beginners and early intermediates. All the chairs are leisurely, light-weight, single-man types (conversations are shouted from chair to chair!). The pistes are either wide motorways or narrow tracks, the latter often too steep to schuss.

APRÈS-SKI

The newly built Oasi centre, beneath a modern church, is the hub of Foppolo's après-ski. It is a conference and promotional centre, but also has a library and gallery. The centre organizes film shows and children's games.

Shopping is rather limited, though standard après-ski is often lively. One of the most popular pizzeria/bars is the Serenella, and afterwards there are discotheques at the hotels Cristallo, Europa and Des Alpes, plus a cinema.

OTHER ACTIVITIES

There is a small (2-km.), easy cross-country loop to the south of the village. Tree cover here, and up on the downhill pistes, is very sparse. The Olympic-size ice rink is floodlit at night, and there is a gymnasium for basket- and volley ball, a covered swimming pool and two bowling alleys. Night toboggan descents are organized.

Though rather isolated for major day-trips it is very much worth taking a trip down the valley to some of the old spa towns such as San Giovanni and San Pellegrino.

LIVIGNO

Access: *Nearest airport:* Milan (6 hrs.). *By road:* N3 motorway, exit Landquart, then via Zernez and Drossa Tunnel. *By rail:* to Tirano, then by bus.

Tourist Office: I-23030 Livigno. Tel. (0342) 99 63 79

Altitude: 1816 m. *Top:* 2800 m.

Language: Italian

Beds: 7,290

Population: 3,600

Health: Doctors in resort. *Hospital:* Samedan (53 km.) and Sondalo (55 km.)

Runs: 85 km.

Lifts: 28

Ski areas: Lago Salin, Monte Sponda, Costaccia

Ski schools: Scuola Italiana di Sci Livigno Inverno/Estate, Scuola Italiana di Sci Interalpen, Scuola Italiana di Sci Livigno Italy, Scuola Italiana di Sci Livigno Soc. Coop.

Linked resorts: None

Season: December to April; summer skiing on Diavolezza glacier

Kindergarten: None

Prices: *Lift pass:* 6 days L. 88,000–120,000 (children L. 70,000–100,000). *Ski school:* Group L. 45,000–55,000 for 6 half-days (children L. 42,000–50,000); private L. 25,000 per hour.

RATINGS

Skiing Conditions	Snow Conditions	For Beginners	For Intermediates	For Advanced Skiers	For Children	Après-Ski	Other Sports	Value for Money
7	8	8	5	5	7	8	2	8

THE RESORT

Livigno is rapidly gaining in popularity, particularly with the British and Swedes, as this is Italy's top duty-free resort. The town itself, once three separate villages, is spread out along a narrow street, without pavements, for nearly 4 km. It appears to be made up largely of grocers selling literally hundreds of brands of alcohol, tobacco, perfume and tea at incredibly low prices (and very little actual food, for those considering an apartment holiday). With a rather spaced-out ski area, Livigno provides an extensive, if not varied, week of ski exploration for the intermediate skier.

Livigno's duty-free status is rumoured to be the result of its inaccessibility. Whenever the government sent out tax collectors, the town helpfully returned them minus their lives. The advent of modern transport hasn't made Livigno much more accessible, with a choice of five-hour transfers from Milan or Zurich (sometimes double that if weather conditions are bad).

THE SKIING

The remarkable thing about Livigno's 28 ski lifts are that 14 of them are approximately 100-m. beginner-drags, down in the valley, mainly stretching up the resort's western side. Yet what might be considered a plus for beginners or families is cancelled out by the fact that by all accounts the ski school hasn't got much going for it, and there isn't a kindergarten or significant discounts for children.

More serious skiing is concentrated in three areas, beneath the Cantone peak (2904 m.) in the south-west, the Costaccia (2368 m.) in the north-west, and over the valley beneath the Della Neve (2785 m.) in the east. The western peaks are linked by a dubious

94

windy ridge-path. It's down to the bottom, a walk across the busy road, then up the other side to reach Della Neve. However, the numerous wide reds make excellent ego-boosting skiing for the progressing intermediate, though more advanced skiers may find the greatest test to their ability in negotiating the bald patches or ice rinks on the runs down to the village (it is possible to ski back to most hotels if you finish the day in the vicinity).

It's best to concentrate a day in each area, because the lifts are poorly laid out and the free ski bus irregular. There's invariably a few sizeable walks in full kit in store, and many people end up satisfied with the area nearest to their accommodation.

Mountain restaurants, like the lifts, are often crowded and vary tremendously in quality. Those off the beaten track are generally better.

APRÈS-SKI

For those interested in a pub crawl, a certain amount of stamina is needed, due to the length of the valley. So it's normally a choice between staying in with the duty-free plonk, going to the local bar or taking a taxi down (or up) to the town centre. However, taxis are mini buses and very cheap and reliable, so this is not a huge problem (they can also be called when the ski bus fails to turn up).

The dispersed layout of the village results in a large number of atmospheric cellar bars and excellent restaurants and pizzerias where the management are noticeably more friendly than usual, and the prices extremely reasonable. The central disco/pub, Foxi's, is guaranteed to be lively every night, and there are two cinemas.

OTHER ACTIVITIES

There is cross-country skiing along the valley, plus a small natural ice rink, tobogganing, and snow scooters for hire. The Hotel du Lac opens its swimming pool to non-residents in the afternoons. St. Moritz is just over the border. There are also regular buses to Bormio, which is included on the lift pass along with Santa Caterina, at no extra cost. Both resorts are good for a skiing day-trip.

MACUGNAGA

Access: *Nearest airport:* Milan (4 hrs.). *By road:* Simplon Tunnel, then via Domodossola. *By rail:* to Domodossola, then by bus.

Tourist Office: I-28030 Macugnaga. Tel. (0324) 65 11 9

Altitude: 1327 m. *Top:* 2900 m.

Language: Italian

Beds: 550 in hotels, 3,500 in apartments and chalets

Population: 700

Health: Doctor in resort. *Hospital:* Domodossola (40 km.)

Runs: 38 km.

Lifts: 12

Ski areas: Belvedere, Passo Moro

Ski schools: Scuola di Sci Macugnaga

Linked resorts: None

Season: December to April

Kindergarten: *Non-ski:* from 3 years. *With ski:* from 5 years

Prices: *Lift pass:* 6 days L. 87,000–103,000. *Ski school:* Group L. 55,000-60,000 for 6 half-days; private L. 23,000 per hour.

RATINGS

Skiing Conditions	Snow Conditions	For Beginners	For Intermediates	For Advanced Skiers	For Children	Après-Ski	Other Sports	Value for Money
8	9	8	9	6	6	7	2	8

THE RESORT

Macugnaga is made up of two pretty villages, Staffa and Pecetto, that have grown together over the kilometre that once separated them. The result is a picturesque, if spaced out, area to the south of Europe's second highest mountain, the Monte Rosa, which divides Italy from Switzerland (Saas-Fee is just over the other side). Staffa is the larger of the two villages, and the hub of shopping and nightlife. Pecetto is slightly more unspoiled, with old buildings mingling with small new hotels.

THE SKIING

The skiing is also divided into two areas, the smaller, Belvedere, above Pecetto, beneath Monte Rosa itself; the larger, Passo Moro, above Staffa. The two areas are linked by a vital ski bus.

The main nursery area (five wide gentle slopes) is served by three drag lifts at the northern edge of Staffa. From here also two cable cars rise in succession, the first to Alpe Bill (the middle station, at 1700 m.), then a long one right up to Passo Moro (the top station, at 2900 m.) where most of the intermediate and advanced skiing is to be found. A choice of four different red or red and black runs descend from top to mid-station, all south-facing on generally wide slopes above the tree line. The views alone from Passo Moro are worth experiencing, and added skiing interest is provided by a further four drag lifts serving a few short reds, black and one blue run. The pistes down to the mid-station suit all standards of intermediate. All are over 5 km. (red) or 3 km. (black) with a vertical drop of 1200 m. The main disappointment is that it is not possible to ski back from the middle cable-car station to the village.

The second, more attractive skiing area is among the trees beneath Belvedere (1932 m.). The top station is reached by two successive chair lifts. There are excellent views from this point. The two runs from top to mid-station are intermediate standard. Below, the pistes are blue or green, and there is an extra drag lift for variety.

Macugnaga enjoys a very long ski season due to good snow conditions, which are helped by its altitude and location. The ski

school normally organizes trips over to Saas-Fee (conditions permitting), and heli-skiing into Switzerland is also possible.

APRÈS-SKI

Famous for good value, Macugnaga has ensured its popularity, especially with the British. There are plenty of cosy little bars and pizzerias. The hub of après-ski activity is around Staffa's village square. Later-evening entertainment is provided by several discotheques, mainly connected to hotels. These include Kiss, Roffel and Big Ben. The atmosphere is quite lively, especially as the local wine is very good—and cheap!

OTHER ACTIVITIES

As you would expect in a rather small resort, there is not much going on. There are natural ice rinks, and toboggans may be hired. Alpine walks are laid out to take maximum advantage of the spectacular scenery. There is one small cross-country loop (4 km.). Excursions later in the season include Lake Como.

MADESIMO

Access: *By air:* Milan (4–5 hrs.). *By road:* N2 motorway to Lugano, then via Menaggio and Chiavenna. *By rail:* to Splügen or Chiavenna, then by bus.

Tourist Office: I-23024 Madesimo sullo Spluga. Tel. (0343) 53 01 5

Altitude: 1550 m. *Top:* 2884 m.

Language: Italian

Beds: 719 in hotels, 6,000 in chalets and apartments

Population: 550

Health: Doctors and fracture clinic in resort. *Hospital:* Chiavenna (20 km.)

Runs: 50 km.

Lifts: 21

Ski areas: Groppera, Val di Lei, Alpe Motta di Campodolcino, Andossi

Ski schools: Scuola Italiana di Sci Madesimo, Scuola Italiana di Sci Valle di Lei

Linked resorts: Motta

Season: End November to end April

Kindergarten: None

Prices: *Lift pass:* 6 days L. 90,000–110,000. *Ski school:* Group L. 70,000 for 6 half-days; private L. 23,000 per hour.

RATINGS

Skiing Conditions	Snow Conditions	For Beginners	For Intermediates	For Advanced Skiers	For Children	Après-Ski	Other Sports	Value for Money
8	8	8	9	8	7	5	3	7

THE RESORT

A higgledy-piggledy mix of ancient farm buildings (some converted into bars and restaurants), and newer, uglier, apartment blocks and hotels are testimony to Madesimo's status as an authentic altitude village, that has expanded, somewhat at random, with the increasing ski traffic. A small river runs through the centre, and the town is criss-crossed by narrow streets containing plenty of little shops, bars and pastry stores.

THE SKIING

For a comparatively small resort, Madesimo's international success has been won on the slopes by the good variety of piste gradient, rare in Italian resorts of this size. Most of the slopes are north-west-facing, with a few to the east. Wide nursery areas are dotted around the resort, with the main one served by the Biancaneve, Gemello and Della Piana lifts. The main altitude skiing at Val di Lei has some nice long gentle runs from the middle cable-car station at Cima del Sole. A special book of lift tickets is available for beginners.

A second cable car takes advanced skiers up to the Pizzo Groppera (2884 m.), from where the famous black Canalone descent drops for 3 km. with a gradient of up to 36°. It takes you through a funnel, down a gorge and emerges above the village. There are other shorter blacks to enjoy, but off-piste is not recommended without first asking the ski school for advice on conditions, preferably taking a guide with you.

Intermediates will enjoy the many reds and blues on this side and over the back of Pizzo Groppera in the Val di Lei. The Colmenetta (2280 m.) lift also offers good intermediate skiing, a little detached from the main area. Much of the skiing is above the tree line, but there is thick wood cover immediately above the resort which makes for enjoyable final descents through the trees back to the village. A good start for such a cruise is Lago Azzurro, a wide sunny area above the resort.

APRÈS-SKI

Usually quite lively and normally good value, with a noticeable British presence midweek, Madesimo has plenty of bars, restaurants and alternative nightspots. A popular stop after skiing is the 200-year-old Osteria Vegia (next to the cable-car station) which is lively for most of the non-skiing hours. If you want to eat in even more traditional surroundings, Dogana Vegia takes you back a further century. The Taverna Verosa cooks pizzas on an open fire. There is a piano cellar bar at La Meridiana, and two popular discotheques, Queen's and the Facsimile Videoteque. Several of the hotels have discotheques, but these are not always open. There's also a cinema.

OTHER ACTIVITIES

There is a large indoor heated swimming pool in the Hotel Cascata, a bowling alley, a natural ice rink floodlit at night and used for ice-hockey matches, and an official toboggan run down to Pianazzo.

Cross-country skiers can enjoy 15 km. of cross-country trails in Madesimo and a further 20 km. in Campodolcino, a 20-minute bus ride away. Excursions are usually arranged to St. Moritz (a very long day-trip in winter) and to Chiavenna, an attractive medieval town 20 km. away.

MADONNA DI CAMPIGLIO

 +

Access: *Nearest airport:* Milan (3½ hrs.). *By road:* A22 motorway, exit San Michele, then via Mezzolombardo and Malè. *By rail:* to Trento, then by bus.

Tourist Office: I-38084 Madonna di Campiglio. Tel. (0465) 42 00 0

Altitude: 1550 m. *Top:* 2500 m.	Ski areas: Cinque Laghi, Spinale, Grostè, Pradalago, Campo Carlo Magno
Language: Italian	
Beds: 30,000	
Population: 1,000	Ski schools: Scuole Italiane di Sci: Madonna di Campiglio, Nazionale, Brenta Alta, Campo Carlo Magno, Cinque Laghi, des Alpes, Cima Tosa
Health: Doctor and fracture clinic in resort. *Hospital:* Tione di Trento (30 km.)	
Runs: 90 km. (150 km. in whole area)	Linked resorts: Folgarida, Marilleva
Lifts: 31	Season: December to April
	Kindergarten: *Non-ski:* none. *With ski:* from 5 years

Prices: *Lift pass:* 6 days L. 135,000–145,000. *Ski school:* Group L. 85,000–100,000 for 6 half-days; private L. 28,000 per hour.

RATINGS

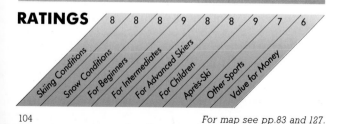

Skiing Conditions	Snow Conditions	For Beginners	For Intermediates	For Advanced Skiers	For Children	Après-Ski	Other Sports	Value for Money
8	8	8	9	8	8	9	7	6

For map see pp.83 and 127.

THE RESORT

At the beginning of the century Santa Maria di Campiglio—as it was then—was rated one of the best summer climbing resorts in the Alps, second only to a few Swiss resorts for ice-climbs, but unbeaten for its rocky Brenta Dolomites scenery. Since 1932 "Campiglio", as it's known by regulars, has been a successful and expanding ski resort, linked by lifts to Marilleva and Folgarida and boasting more than 150 km. of piste. Now a bustling town with a modern central complex and plenty of facilities, Campiglio is slightly chic and popular with the Italians who make up the vast majority of its clientele.

THE SKIING

Skiing is possible in almost every direction from Campiglio, with no less than four cable cars from village level. To the south-east a long télécabine leaves Campo Carlo Mango, a 10-minute bus ride from the resort, and takes you to Passo del Grostè, the highest skiing at 2500 m. The runs back are long, blue, often busy but very enjoyable cruises—assuming the bitter winds that cut across the exposed area above the trees aren't blowing. Lower down, the piste narrows to a long path down through the firs, and from here a few red options open up.

Another south-east ascent is possible on the small, old-fashioned Spinale car which departs 100 m. from the centre of town and usually attracts queues, even off peak-season. From here the runs are very different from those from Grostè, shorter but steep in comparison. The Grostè skiing can also be reached by a long chair from near the top of Spinale.

The south-west is covered by the Pancugolo cable car (to 2070 m.), with a further lift taking you up to 2125 m. and the start of the popular 3-Tre (or "Tre Tre") piste, which is also the World Cup run and the only one featuring snow-making facilities. Quite a steep red, especially by Campiglio's standards, it is linked to several blacks or alternative reds.

Out of Campiglio another cable car ascends to Pradalago (2100 m.). From here an easy red and a chair take you to Monte Vigo (2179 m.) and the descents to Marilleva (1400 m.) due north,

or Folgarida (1270 m.). Marilleva and Folgarida are covered by
most variations of the lift pass, and some combinations also offer
Pinzolo in the Val di Sole beyond them. But look carefully at the
separate sections for information on local skiing to these resorts.

Back in Campiglio, nursery slopes are scattered around the
village outskirts and are generally good.

There are numerous alternative lifts (usually chairs) to all the
areas mentioned. Only a third of the total number of lifts are
drags. Therefore a good choice of resort for those who like to sit
down between descents. Many of the pistes are carved through
the trees, above which the Brenta Dolomites are particularly
spectacular.

Campiglio's skiing is extensive and offers plenty of daily
alternatives for the intermediate and advancing skier. It's generally best to stick to one area a day.

APRÈS-SKI

There is a slightly chic atmosphere in Campiglio. The old centre has some attractive architecture, the new precinct is well laid out, and both areas are packed with shops selling largely luxury or high quality goods. There are also plenty of piano bars, tea bars and a colourful ice-cream parlour. Later on you might explore numerous night spots: the Stork Club combines pizzeria, restaurant, discotheque and "country club", whilst Contrasto is content just to be a trendy discotheque.

When you tire of the slopes, you can always go shopping for après-ski wear.

OTHER ACTIVITIES

The total length of cross-country loops is 30 km., the best organized being at Campo Carlo Magno which is a special centre. The competition trails are Malga Mondifra and Malga Dare. There is an indoor swimming pool, high-speed Olympic ice circuit, ice motor-biking, and 5000 sq. m. of ice rink on the frozen lake. The ski schools offer tuition in all the new snow sports, especially surf.

Campiglio is well placed on the borders of Val Rendena and the Val di Sole for excursions to towns like Trento, Bolzano or Verona—even Venice is sometimes offered. In the village itself, there are plans to repeat a film festival held in early March 1988 which brought highlights from Hollywood's history to the cinema. Theatrical and cabaret productions are occasionally staged.

MARILLEVA

Access: *Nearest airport:* Verona (3 hrs.); Milan (5 hrs.). *By road:* A22 motorway, exit San Michele, then via Ponte Mostizzolo. *By rail:* to Malè, then by bus.

Tourist Office: I-38020 Mezzana-Marilleva. Tel. (0463) 77 13 4

Altitude: 900/1400 m. *Top:* 2179 m.	Ski areas: Doss della Pesa, Monte Vigo
Language: Italian	Ski schools: Scuola Italiana di Sci Marilleva Commezzadura
Beds: 1,600 in hotels, 7,000 in chalets and apartments	
	Linked resorts: Folgarida, Madonna di Campiglio
Population: 800	
Health: Doctors in resort. *Hospital:* Cles (20 km.)	Season: Mid-December to mid-April
Runs: 40 km. (150 km. in whole area)	Kindergarten: *Non-ski:* none. *With ski:* from 4 years
Lifts: 11	

Prices: *Lift pass:* 7 days L. 135,000–150,000 (children L. 115,000–120,000). *Ski school:* Group L. 65,000–70,000 for 6 half-days; private L. 30,000 per hour.

RATINGS

Skiing Conditions	Snow Conditions	For Beginners	For Intermediates	For Advanced Skiers	For Children	Après-Ski	Other Sports	Value for Money
8	8	7	9	8	6	4	4	6

For map see pp. 83 and 127.

THE RESORT

There are essentially two Marillevas, distinguished by their heights. The main "resort", at 1400 m., is a collection of stylish, purpose-built, low-profile apartments and sports hotels, with the ski lifts converging in the centre. Marilleva 900—made up of rectangular blocks reminiscent of a motorway services area—is situated off the main road along the Val di Sole floor and is linked to the mother ship by a prehistoric bucket lift that takes more than 15 minutes to reach 1400 m. and is exceptionally difficult to get on and off, doubly so when wearing ski boots and carrying skis and poles.

THE SKIING

In the north-west corner of the Brenta Dolomites, the peaks become more regular and traditional Alpine slopes are more in evidence. Marilleva, together with Folgarida and Madonna di Campiglio, form one of Italy's largest ski circuits, with more than 150 km. of varied piste. For beginners this may start on a nursery slope by Marilleva 900, but the chances of adequate snow cover at this altitude are remote during much of the season, necessitating a bucket lift ride to Marilleva 1400, where a wide nursery area allows adequate space for serious falling over in the early days. Snow-making facilities on this and the main blue piste back down to the resort should ensure good conditions.

The Copai télécabine heads south from Marilleva 1400 to below Doss della Pesa. From here two further chairs take you to Monte Vigo—the crossroads for resort-hoppers. If you head straight on south down a red then up one more chair, you arrive at Pradalago (2100 m.), directly above Madonna di Campiglio, centre for more than half of the area's skiing, including the most challenging. Do a V-turn off to the north-east to descend towards Folgarida.

Marilleva's own section of the skiing is entirely north-facing and includes a steepish but relatively easy black back from Doss della Pesa to Marilleva 1400. The top point can also be reached by successive chair lifts from 1400 itself.

Crowds tend to develop at the major access lifts between resorts. Officially there is not much variety in the runs, but unofficial trails develop into steep mogul descents.

Most ski pass combinations cover Folgarida and Madonna di Campiglio, as well as neighbouring Pinzolo beyond Madonna di Campiglio to the south, and Pejo to the north. Neither of the last two are ski linked, nor really worth undue effort as the skiing at both is limited, but they are within 45 minutes' drive in either direction.

APRÈS-SKI

A favourite non-skiing pastime is sunbathing: the balconies of the apartment blocks are designed as suntraps and are usually filled with recumbent sun-worshippers. Après-ski is normally centred on local facilities, but around 1400 there are several discos and further down (at about 1300 m.) the Lores disco and pub. Otherwise the blocks have all you need under one roof. Although there is very little to do in Marilleva 900, there is a games room and cellar disco bar for clients of the Hotel Marilleva 900. The small, original non-skiing village of Mezzana, which offers a little variety, is ten minutes' walk away.

OTHER ACTIVITIES

Cross-country trails depart from near Marilleva 900 to neigh-bouring Commezzadura (2 km.), along the valley floor (snow permitting). In addition, there is ski mountaineering, a swimming pool with sauna and solarium at both resorts (500 m. away from Marilleva 900 at the Lago Rotondo Sports Complex), darts, heli-skiing (at 1400 m.) and horse riding.

MONTE BONDONE

Access: *Nearest airport:* Milan (3½ hrs.); Verona (1½ hrs.). *By road:* A22 motorway to Trento. *By rail:* to Trento, then by bus. Tourist Office: I-38100 Trento. Tel. (0461) 98 38 80

Altitude: 984 m. *Top:* 2098 m.	Ski areas: La Rosta, Montesel
Language: Italian	Ski schools: Scuola di Sci Monte Bondone-Trento
Beds: 1,253	
Population: 200	Linked resorts: None
Health: Hospital and fracture clinic in Trento	Season: December to April
	Kindergarten: *Non-ski:* none. *With ski:* 3–10 years.
Runs: 10 km.	
Lifts: 8	

Prices: *Lift pass:* 7 days L. 80,600–90,000. *Ski school:* Group L. 64,000 for 6 half-days; private L. 25,000 per hour.

RATINGS

Skiing Conditions	Snow Conditions	For Beginners	For Intermediates	For Advanced Skiers	For Children	Après-Ski	Other Sports	Value for Money
7	7	8	4	2	6	4	2	7

THE RESORT

Monte Bondone isn't a resort as such but the mountain on which the skiing takes place. There are a number of small villages around the slopes, but realistically this is "Trento's mountain"—the destination of skiing commuters from the region's capital city.

Where you base yourself is a matter for debate. Trento itself is only a 30-minute drive from the slopes, and is a good choice for those with their own car, as the roads up the mountain are kept clear of snow. Thus, you have the benefit of both city facilities and skiing. It's almost similar to an Innsbruck-based holiday on the other side of the Brenner Pass (though without the extent of the skiing). Many of the main hotels in Trento provide complimentary travel to the ski areas.

The first major village up the mountain road is Sardagna, only 15 minutes from Trento. For the less mobile, this is a good compromise, as a bus takes you up to the resort, whilst a cable car leaves from just beneath the village and descends over motorway and river to arrive near the railway lines in Trento itself. Candriai (984 m.) is less than 10 minutes from the bottom lift and is a larger village. The three resorts by the slopes proper are Vaneze (1300 m.), Norge (1400 m.) and Vason (1650 m.).

Vaneze seems most popular with British operators and is linked to Vason by bucket lift. None of the three can really be called villages, they are just collections of hotels and the odd bar.

114

THE SKIING

The skiing is even more limited than one might originally think, since the most exciting 5 km. of piste is only open at weekends and in high season when the population of Trento naturally migrates to the slopes. The area is best for beginners, second-week skiers or someone looking for a town base with the odd day's skiing thrown in and who is not too bothered about après-ski atmosphere. You also get the bonus of not paying excessively for lifts you might not use.

The day begins with a bit of an uphill walk if you're anywhere but Vaneze. Even there it's likely you'll have a walk to either the chair taking you to a spot below Montesel (1729 m.), or to the long, standing bucket ride (14–18 minutes) up to Vason. Ski school and the nursery area are located here, the latter served by a single drag and away from the main skiing. This is quite pleasant, very wide and surrounded by bars in which to make those emergency

stops. All the other lifts in the resort are chairs; one rises from Vason to Monte Palon, at 2098 m. the area's highest skiing. All the other lifts stop at the ridge peaked by Monte Palon, where there's nothing but a very steep drop and spectacular views of the Trento valley beyond.

A 500-m. blackish piste runs from Palon, turning red at the top of the other, shorter chair from Vason. The most interesting run is a long 5-km. red down to Malga Mezavia (1170 m.), and split in two by the pass road. Two chairs take you back up, but only in high season, since snow conditions may deteriorate later on. There are a couple more chairs running parallel up to Montesel, the base station situated midway between Vaneze and Vason (1650 m.). All the skiing in this sector is blue. Apart from the last few hundred metres of the Rocce Rosse run, all the skiing is above the tree line.

APRÈS-SKI

As you've probably surmised, après-ski is very limited. Evening meals are best taken in your hotel, followed by a drink at the hotel bar and a trip down to the Studio 1 discotheque (if staying in Vaneze) or Disco Shock in Vason. Tour operators will organize additional activities.

OTHER ACTIVITIES

Cross-country skiers will enjoy three loops beyond Vason, at a reasonably high altitude (over 1540 m.). These are a small green and two medium-length blue and red trails, all above the tree line. Ski school teaches mono and surf skiing; toboggans may be hired. There is a natural ice rink with brush ice hockey available. Excursions are usually organized to Lake Garda over the valley and to Venice (the winter months are often the best time to visit the latter).

If you're down in Trento, there's obviously a wealth of sightseeing opportunities: the 12th-century Palazzo Pretorio, housing the Diocesan Museum; the cathedral (from the 12th and 13th centuries); Via Belenzani, lined with Renaissance palaces; the 15th-century Chiesa di Santa Maria Maggiore; and the Castello di Buonconsiglio's art museum.

ORTISEI-ST. ULRICH

 +

Access: *Nearest airport:* Munich (5 hrs.). *By road:* A22 motorway, exit Chiusa, then via Gröden. *By rail:* to Chiusa or Bolzano, then by bus.

Tourist Office: I-39046 Ortisei-St. Ulrich. Tel. (0471) 76 32 8

Altitude: 1236 m. *Top:* 2518 m.	Ski areas: Seceda, Alpe di Siusi, Rasciesa
Language: Italian, German and Ladin	Ski schools: Scuola di Sci Ortisei
Beds: 6,300	
Population: 4,500	Linked resorts: Arabba, Campitello, Canazei, Colfosco, Corvara, San Cassiano, Santa Cristina, Selva, La Villa
Health: Doctors in resort. *Hospital:* Bressanone/Brixen (29 km.)	
	Season: December to April
Runs: 175 km. in Val Gardena	Kindergarten: *Non-ski:* from 2½ years. *With ski:* from 3–8 years
Lifts: 6 (85 in Val Gardena)	

Prices: *Lift pass:* 6 days L. 122,000–147,100 (children L. 85,900–103,300). *Ski school:* L. 80,000 for 3 days; private L. 27,000 per hour.

RATINGS

Skiing Conditions	Snow Conditions	For Beginners	For Intermediates	For Advanced Skiers	For Children	Après-Ski	Other Sports	Value for Money
8	8	8	9	7	6	7	5	7

THE RESORT

As Selva is Wolkenstein, so Ortisei is St. Ulrich—the title the village held for several centuries before the South Tyrol, of which it is a part, came under Italian rule after World War I. Most signposts give both names, and the Austrian Tyrolean influence remains very strong. It has a charming old town, decorated with ice sculptures and is marginally more attractive than its more famous neighbour, Selva. Prices tend to be lower here, too.

THE SKIING

Ortisei lies just a few kilometres from Selva and Santa Cristina. It's possible to ski to many other resorts, also covered by the Dolomiti Superski pass. These include Corvara, Arabba and La Villa, but the Sella Ronda circuit on which the resorts are situated is further from Ortisei than Selva.

The highest point on the north side, Seceda (2518 m.) is the start of several runs, largely reds, served by a few drags, which may be followed down to either village. The main skiing on Alpe di Siusi is reached by a single cable car to Punta Mesdi (2005 m.), from where the runs sink slowly into a huge tree-free snow bowl. The pistes are mainly easy, but there are a few short reds around the edge, notably from Punta d'Oro (2238 m.) and Alpe Bullaccia (2125 m.)—the highest points.

It's another two-stage cable car from Alpe di Siusi running north-west which links with Santa Cristina, Selva and thence into the Sella Ronda. Though more advanced skiers reach extensive ski areas, they might consider staying further up the valley.

The area is an excellent place for beginners and, unlike most altitude ski areas, is covered by bars, restaurants and hotels. A ski bus runs between Selva and Ortisei, through Santa Cristina.

APRÈS-SKI

Ortisei is quite a sizeable resort, with plenty of bars, cafés and restaurants, plus cinema. There is one discotheque or, alternatively, dancing to live music. Concerts are organized occasionally, and there are folklore evenings and films.

OTHER ACTIVITIES

Ortisei is also popular with cross-country skiers, who can go from Siusi right across to Montepana above Santa Cristina. There are

other loops between the two resorts, down in the valley. There is an ice-skating rink (popular local ice-hockey league), a large covered indoor pool, a small heated outdoor pool, bowling and toboggan runs, plus tennis, squash and horse riding.

The museum of local history houses displays of religious wood-carving. In fact, Ortisei is famed for its wood-carving industry (the same is true of Selva and Santa Cristina), and visitors are welcome in most shops to watch the craftsmen and -women at work. It is also worth a visit to the Chiesa di San Antonio (1676) and the even older Chiesa di San Giacomo (1181) with exquisite Gothic frescoes from the 14th century.

A sleigh-ride up on the Alpe di Siusi is an enjoyable experience, affording splendid views if you take time off your skiing to make the trip in daylight.

Lacy balconies, façades painted with rustic scenes—small touches that lend charm to Ortisei architecture.

PASSO TONALE

 +

Access: *Nearest airport:* Milan (3 hrs.). *By road:* A4 motorway to Bergamo. *By rail:* to Edolo, then by bus.

Tourist Office: I-25056 Passo Tonale. Tel. (0364) 91 34 3.

Altitude: 1883 m. *Top:* 3016 m.	Lifts: 20
Language: Italian	Ski areas: Tonale, Presena
Beds: 1,600 in hotels, 4,000 in apartments	Ski schools: Scuola di Sci Pirovano, Scuola di Sci Miramonti
Population: 200	Linked resorts: Ponte di Legno
Health: Doctor and fracture clinic in Tonale. *Hospital:* Edolo (30 km.)	Season: October to May
	Kindergarten: *Non-ski:* from 4 years. *With ski:* none, but ski school from 5 years
Runs: 80 km.	

Prices: *Lift pass:* 6 days L. 97,000–115,000 (children L. 75,000–92,000). *Ski school:* Group L. 60,000–65,000 for 6 half-days; private L. 25,000 per hour.

RATINGS

Skiing Conditions	Snow Conditions	For Beginners	For Intermediates	For Advanced Skiers	For Children	Après-Ski	Other Sports	Value for Money
8	9	8	7	6	6	7	5	7

See also map p. 83.

THE RESORT

Tonale sits on the pass between the Trento and Lombardy regions of northern Italy. Situated south of Bormio and north of Madonna di Campiglio (both of which are within an hour or so's drive), it's one of Italy's highest ski resorts, but a traditional village, not purpose-built. It is possible to ski or take a bus down to Ponte di Legno, the larger, neighbouring village down the valley. The mountains above are distinctly Alpine, as opposed to the Dolomites' famous pink crags and precipices to the south.

THE SKIING

Tonale provides plenty of skiing for the beginner and intermediate. First-timers especially benefit from a massive nursery area, below Valbiolo (2244 m.), which can afford to be right next to the resort because its height is so snow-sure. The slopes here are south-facing, and as Tonale is situated in a wide, open valley, the area enjoys a maximum of sunshine.

Though most of the runs are green or blue, there are two blacks from the Paradiso cable-car top station (and a blue for those who change their minds at the top). When you're down in Ponte di Legno, there's a further black from Corno d'Aola (1920 m.).

The Paradiso cable car takes you up to the Presena glacier, a summer-skiing area which opens up in March. The glacier area is "over the border" from the Trento region and is officially situated in Brescia. Glacier lifts, when open, should be included in the normal lift pass. The glacier is sheltered and there are no crevasses.

Elsewhere on the winter slopes are some exceptionally long runs, including the popular off-piste Pisgana slope, a full 15 km. The Cantiere is 16 km. and Vescasa 9 km. in length, both also officially off-piste. A ski bus links Tonale with Ponte di Legno. Most of the Ponte di Legno slopes have snow-making facilities. You can ski from Tonale to Ponte di Legno, but the return trip must be made by ski bus.

APRÈS-SKI

Ponte di Legno is the larger village, with the lion's share of facilities and après-ski variety, as well as shopping; but there's still a good selection of hotel bars in Tonale itself. There's little potential for those wanting to eat out. Tonale at least has four discotheques. Most are connected to hotels, and the most popular is probably the Embassy Club. Down in Ponte di Legno, another couple of discos include the delightfully titled Funny Hell.

OTHER ACTIVITIES

There are 15 km. of cross-country trails in the valley. The swimming pool offers free entry to those with a lift-pass ticket valid for more than two days; and the Hotel Mirella also has a swimming pool. There are dog sleds, an ice-skating rink, tobogganing, and a billiards hall. For the adventurous, there are two ski jumps—35 m. and 52 m. Excursions are normally organized to Madonna di Campiglio, Trento, Bolzano and St. Moritz.

PEJO

Access: *Nearest airport:* Verona (2½ hrs.); Milan (4 hrs.). *By road:* A22 motorway, exit Bolzano or San Michele, then via Malè. *By rail:* to Trento or Mezzacorona, then private line to Malè and bus.

Tourist Office: I-38020 Pejo. Tel. (0463) 73 10 0

Altitude: 900/1400 m.
Top: 2400 m.

Language: Italian

Beds: 3,100

Population: 20

Health: Doctor in resort.
Hospital: Cles (40 km.)

Runs: 15 km.

Lifts: 7

Ski areas: Pian di Laret

Ski schools: Scuola Italiana di Sci Pejo, Scuola Italiana di Sci 13 Cime

Linked resorts: None

Season: December to April

Kindergarten: None

Prices: *Lift pass:* 7 days L. 85,000–120,000 (children L. 70,000–80,000). *Ski school:* Group L. 45,000–50,000 for 6 half-days; private L. 22,000 per hour.

RATINGS

Skiing Conditions	Snow Conditions	For Beginners	For Intermediates	For Advanced Skiers	For Children	Après-Ski	Other Sports	Value for Money
6	7	7	7	5	6	4	1	7

THE RESORT

Pejo Fonti (1340 m.) and Pejo Paese (1585 m.) lie side by side at the top of the Val di Sole in the Trento region. This takes in the western half of the main Dolomites massif, together with the Brenta Dolomites to the west of the main group—and at the north of which we find Pejo, linked with Cogolo (1160 m.), the main village on the valley floor before you ascend to Pejo proper.

THE SKIING

Pejo does not have an extensive ski area. There are just six lifts, plus a baby drag in Cogolo, and eight pistes totalling 15 km. In short, this is not a place for the expert. On the other hand three of the runs are red (two blues) and the Tarlenta run, from the cable-car top station, winds down through the trees for 4 km. initially, but if the snow is deep enough you can ski right down to the valley. When the snow is scarce at Pejo Fonti, there's artificial snow for the last half-kilometre of this run.

Higher up, skiing extends via two chair lifts to an altitude of 2800 m. The two runs from here drop nearly 500 m. to the Pian di Laret (2340 m.), giving the advanced intermediate plenty to think about.

Intermediate skiers will find enough in Pejo for a couple of days, and can—with own transport—spend the rest of the time down at the 150-km. area offered by the resorts of Folgarida, Marilleva and Madonna di Campiglio just down the valley. Beginners will find a good nursery area in Pejo, with very reasonable prices for instruction.

Folgarida and Marilleva are covered by the ''Skirama'' lift pass, but Madonna di Campiglio may not be (depending on pass conditions at the time of your visit), in which case an extension pass will be needed.

APRÈS-SKI

Pejo Fonti is an old spa town where one can still take the waters. There is a good range of hotels, all of which have bars open to the public. Otherwise, there is very little for the winter tourist. Hotel bars make up the majority of the nightlife, with one discotheque and some pizzerias.

OTHER ACTIVITIES

There is a cross-country skiers' loop and ski school down in Cogolo, but make sure there's snow in the valley before booking. There are also natural ice rinks in Pejo Fonti and Cogolo, a swimming pool in Pejo Fonti and horse riding in Cogolo. A fitness trail has been established for orienteering with compass and map. Excursions to Bolzano, Trento, Verona, Venice or down the Val di Sole to Madonna di Campiglio are all possible.

PILA

 +

Access: *Nearest airport:* Turin (2 hrs.). *By road:* A5 motorway to Aosta. *By rail:* to Aosta, then by bus.

Tourist Office: I-11020 Pila. Tel. (0165) 52 10 00

Altitude: 1790 m. *Top:* 2620 m.	Lifts: 12
Language: Italian	Ski areas: La Noura, Lago Leissé, Grand Grimod
Beds: 1,230 in hotels, 1,280 in apartments	Ski schools: Scuola di Sci Pila
Population: 20	Linked resorts: None
Health: Doctor and fracture clinic in resort. *Hospital:* Aosta (19 km.)	Season: December to April
	Kindergarten: *Non-ski:* from 1 year. *With ski:* from 4 years
Runs: 70 km.	

Prices: *Lift pass:* 6 days L. 133,000–142,000. *Ski school:* Group L. 95,000 for 6 half-days; private L. 25,000 per hour.

RATINGS

Skiing Conditions	Snow Conditions	For Beginners	For Intermediates	For Advanced Skiers	For Children	Après-Ski	Other Sports	Value for Money
7	7	6	7	6	6	7	1	7

THE RESORT

Like La Thuile and indeed many Italian resorts, Pila is an old town having undergone considerable recent expansion. In this instance, five new apartment block/hotel developments have dramatically improved facilities.

THE SKIING

The skiing is substantial for a relatively small resort. Lifts are constantly being built or improved; three new chair lifts are due to open in December 1988. The ski area stretches in a huge half-bowl above the resort, with trees lining the pistes to 2300 m., a boon when visibility is less than perfect. The lifts usually begin a few hundred metres from any accommodation, though a bus service does link those places with a longer walk to the lifts. To the east, a chair lift will take you to Chamolé from where several reds descend through the trees including a FIS homologated downhill run to Plan Pra.

Beginners are catered for with nursery slopes in the village and at the Grand Grimod area, reached by cable car to the west of the resort. Ski school prices seem to have been set in advance of the expansion the resort clearly envisages, though lessons are normally four hours per day (instead of two). Snow-making facilities will be introduced in November 1988.

APRÈS-SKI

With the numerous new apartment blocks and hotels have come a good selection of shops, restaurants, pizzerias and bars. The resort seems to be building accommodation madly and indeed extending its skiing in preparation for a sudden vast increase in tourists. Though Pila is by no means a ghost resort, it is also rarely overflowing and so the number of bars and restaurants, if anything, seem too many. There's certainly plenty to do in the evenings, and a choice of three discotheques to round them off in.

OTHER ACTIVITIES

There is one 5-km. cross-country ski loop, plus a skating rink, solarium in hotels and massage. Sightseeing in nearby Aosta (19 km.) is a must. Parts of this Roman town are more than 2,000 years old. Access is easy as there is a gondola connection.

PINZOLO

Access: *Nearest airport:* Verona (2½ hrs.); Milan (3½ hrs.). *By road:* A22 motorway to Trento, then via Sarche. *By rail:* to Trento, then by bus.

Tourist Office: I-38086 Pinzolo. Tel. (0465) 51 00 7

Altitude: 800 m. *Top:* 2100 m.	Ski areas: Doss del Sabion, Alpe di Grual
Language: Italian	
Beds: 12,000	Ski schools: Scuola Italiana di Sci Pinzolo, Scuola Italiana di Sci Nardis
Population: 3,000	
Health: Doctor in resort. *Hospital:* Tione di Trento (15 km.)	Linked resorts: None
	Season: December to April
Runs: 30 km.	Kindergarten: *Non-ski:* none. *With ski:* from 3 years
Lifts: 9	

Prices: *Lift pass:* 6 days L. 76,000–88,000. *Ski school:* Group L. 60,000-85,000 for 7 half-days; private L. 25,000 per hour.

RATINGS

Skiing Conditions	Snow Conditions	For Beginners	For Intermediates	For Advanced Skiers	For Children	Après-Ski	Other Sports	Value for Money
8	8	8	8	6	7	7	5	8

THE RESORT

Situated low in the Brenta Dolomites and in the middle of the Adamello Brenta National Park, Pinzolo is a genuine old village, developing towards a planned ski lift link with Madonna di Campiglio 13 km. up the valley. Despite its low altitude, Pinzolo has a good snow record and in any case the main skiing area is quickly reached by a modern high-speed télécabine from the village outskirts. Summer tourism began here just after the war, the first ski lifts being installed in 1970. The local people are especially friendly. Pinzolo offers a good base for the beginner or intermediate skier.

THE SKIING

The resort's six-seater télécabine blasts off from the top end of the village and takes you up to Pra Rotondo (1550 m.), where nursery slopes are served by a single drag lift. From here most people prefer to go straight up to the top—Doss del Sabion (2100 m.). The old but pleasant one-man chair making this link is due to be replaced for the 88/89 season by a fast four-man, which should relieve occasional high-season queues that tend to build up at this point. Most of the time the skiing is remarkably uncrowded.

There is the option of taking the blue back down to Pinzolo (conditions permitting, of course—realistically the chances of snow down to the resort are remote these days). Alternatively, you can continue upwards from Pra Rotondo or take the Fossadei, Broc and Cioca chairs and drags across the main area, with some short blue runs in between. The meeting point of these lifts and the

run from Doss del Sabion is Alpe di Grual, where Pinzolo's most popular descents "Grual Nera" and "Grual Rossa" start—"nera" meaning black and "rossa" red. In reality they are both part of a huge snow basin, the only treeless area (at the top), which can be skied at virtually any angle. Apart from a black above Pra Rotondo, the piste is mainly intermediate standard. Those with understanding insurers, however, might care to try numerous steep unofficial mogul-fields which develop below the chair lifts. There is also plenty of opportunity for off-piste between the trees. The descent from top station to resort (conditions permitting) of either all blue, or black and blue pistes, is extremely enjoyable.

The weekly ski passes can include one or two days each in Madonna di Campiglio and Folgarida or Marilleva, a 30-minute bus ride away.

APRÈS-SKI

Although Pinzolo has clearly benefited from the ski business, it is quite a substantial village in its own right with a comparatively large resident population—a good place for shopping, with craft, fashion and sports shops, as well as a small high-quality department store and various specialized boutiques.

There are plenty of bars, both in hotels and out. One of the most popular with the young is the Ciclamino, above a discotheque of the same name—complete with big video screen. This same complex houses the tourist office and a library. There are other discotheques and cellar dancing bars, notably the one at the Hotel Pinzolo-Dolomiti. There are also ice-cream parlours and wine bars, but restaurants outside hotels are hard to find.

OTHER ACTIVITIES

Cross-country skiing is a speciality in Pinzolo. The floodlit 2½-km. circuit is the stage for a mass-entry, international, 24-hour race held in early February with accompanying festivities. A further 10 km. of trails are available beyond the competition circuit.

The Rendena Valley riding school offers lessons for beginners, cross-country riding or jumping. There's a large public indoor pool at Spiazzo Rendena, 3 km., and an ice rink where curling and ice-hockey competitions are held. On the slopes you can toboggan or walk along prepared trails at resort level.

Be warned that a 6-km. trek to the (not-so-well-signposted) Nardis waterfall is not such a good idea in winter. The walk is pleasant enough but the waterfall needs the spring melt water to reach its acclaimed "spectacular" proportions. The café there is closed in winter, too. More leisurely coach excursions are arranged to Madonna di Campiglio, Trento, Verona and Venice.

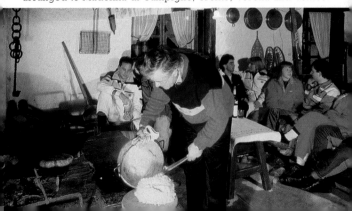

SAN MARTINO DI CASTROZZA

Access: *Nearest airport:* Venice (2½–3 hrs.); Milan (6 hrs.). *By road:* A22 motorway, exit Ora, then via Pedrazzo. *By rail:* to Ora, then by bus.

Tourist Office: I-38058 S. Martino di Castrozza. Tel. (0439) 68 10 1

Altitude: 1450 m. *Top:* 2741 m.	Ski areas: Alpe di Tognola, Malga Ces, Rif. Col Verde-Rosetta
Language: Italian, German	
Beds: 2,734 in hotels, 9,500 in apartments	Ski schools: Scuola Italiana di Sci San Martino di Castrozza, Scuola di Sci Sass Maor-Primiero
Population: 600	
Health: Doctor in resort. *Hospital:* Feltre (47 km.)	Linked resorts: None
Runs: 50 km.	Season: Beginning December to mid-April
Lifts: 24	
	Kindergarten: None

Prices: *Lift pass:* 6 days L. 131,000 (children L. 98,000). *Ski school:* Group L. 65,000 for 6 half-days; private L. 27,000 per hour.

RATINGS

Skiing Conditions	Snow Conditions	For Beginners	For Intermediates	For Advanced Skiers	For Children	Après-Ski	Other Sports	Value for Money
7	8	8	8	7	7	7	6	7

See also map p. 14–15.

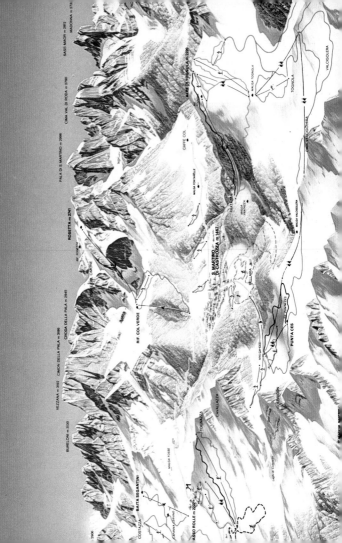

BURELON m 3130 VEZZANA m 3192 CIMON DELLA PALA m 3186 CRODA DELLA PALA m 2945 ROSETTA m 2741 PALA DI S.MARTINO m 2986 CIMA VAL DI RODA m 2790 SASS MAOR m 2812 MADONNA m 2731

BAITA SEGANTINI

ASSO ROLLE m 2222

COSTAZZA

MALGA FOSSE

CATINACCIO

CAVALLAZZA

TOGNAZZA

CORONCON

COLBRICON

PUNTA CES

MALGA CES

Laghi di Colbricon

BELLAVISTA

S. MARTINO
DI CASTROZZA m 1467

MALGA CROSETTA

PRATI PIERI

MALGA FRADUSTA

MALGA VALCIGOLERA

CIMA VALCIGOLERA

TOGNOLA

MALGA TOGNOLA

ALPE DI TOGNOLA m 2220

VALCIGOLERA

VALDGOLERA

RIF.COL VERDE

VAL CIGADA

MALGA FONTANELLE

CIAFFE COL

1906

THE RESORT

The spectacular mountain backdrop of the Pal di San Martino gives visitors to this Southern Dolomites resort an added bonus. Not to be confused with the Dolomites' other San Martino, just south of San Vigilio, this is quite a large though not especially attractive village, with the majority of activity around the old church. Ski lifts surround the village, but are a little way outside, so several of the hotels provide a courtesy mini-bus in addition to the regular ski bus service.

THE SKIING

Though part of the Dolomiti Superski scheme, San Martino is not linked to any of the other resorts. It has 50 km. of its own pistes, currently scattered around the resort, roughly divided into three main areas. Each is served initially by chair and/or cable-car ascents, starting some distance from the village centre.

The ski bus runs to the Malga Ces area where three drags serve nursery slopes. From the area's top point, Punta Ces, two average reds and a narrow black descend, but it's worth stopping a few moments to take in the view across San Martino to the sheer cliff faces of the mountains beyond.

The second area, beneath Alpe di Tognola (2220 m.) is reached by a ten-minute ski-bus ride from the village to the bottom lift, or by a long chair-lift link from Malga Ces. From the top of Alpe di Tognola there's a choice of blue descents (with the option of more blues or lower reds served by drags) to the bottom télécabine station at Fratazza. The black runs beneath the télécabine for much of its distance—most embarrassing to wipe out on this one!

The third area rises to Rif. Col Verde by chair lift from the other side of the village. One fairly easy red cuts down through the trees and a single drag takes you back up if you change your mind half way. More interestingly, the resort's only cable car runs from Rif. Col Verde to the highest accessible point, Rosetta at 2741 m. At the top there is a simple, short blue, with its own drag lift. It is possible only for experts to ski down to Rif. Col Verde, but even they should definitely enlist the help of a guide as there are no marked pistes.

A free ski bus also runs to the neighbouring, high-altitude resort of Passo Rolle (2222 m.), 9 km. away. Here five drag and two chair lifts serve a selection of green, blue, red and black runs (virtually unconnected).

Back in San Martino, beginners have a choice of six unlinked nursery slopes, each with its own drag. Three run parallel to each other by the village beneath Rif. Col Verde, the others, as mentioned, beneath Malga Ces.

APRÈS-SKI

Despite its size, San Martino retains the atmosphere of smaller Italian resorts, with much of its nightlife confined to hotel bars. Very Italian, like the majority of visitors, the village is popular with families who just enjoy a stroll around the shops before returning to their apartments. There are, however, a number of good discotheques (Cimone and Tabia), together with a wide selection of restaurants serving a full range of Alpine favourites from fondue to pizza. The Drei Tannen restaurant is one of the resort's best, whilst the English Pub is usually lively into the small hours. There's also a cinema.

OTHER ACTIVITIES

Cross-country skiers have green and red circuits in San Martino, with a long black loop in Passo Rolle which is pretty snow-sure. San Martino has a special cross-country ski centre with instructors, maintenance facilities, changing rooms and refreshments. There's a natural ice rink, a 15-minute walk out of the centre of the village, horse riding, bowling, and an indoor swimming pool in La Vecchia Fornace centre.

SANSICARIO

Access: *Nearest airport:* Turin (2 hrs.). *By road:* Fréjus Tunnel, then via Bardonecchia. *By rail:* to Oulx, then by bus.

Tourist Office: I-10054 Cesana. Tel. (0122) 81 11 75

Altitude: 1200 m. *Top:* 2700 m.

Language: Italian

Beds: 5,000

Population: 30

Health: Doctor and fracture clinic in resort. *Hospital:* Briançon (34 km.) or Susa (40 km.)

Runs: 38 km. (Milky Way 300 km.)

Lifts: 13 (Milky Way 100)

Ski areas: Fraiteve, Monti della Luna

Ski schools: Scuola di Sci Sansicario-Cesana

Linked resorts: Claviere, Cesana Torinese, Grangesises, Montgenèvre (France)

Season: December to end April

Kindergarten: *Non-ski:* 3–13 years *With ski:* 3–13 years

Prices: *Lift pass:* 6 days L. 130,000–140,000. *Ski school:* Group 100,000–120,000 for 6 half-days; private L. 26,000 per hour.

RATINGS

Skiing Conditions	Snow Conditions	For Beginners	For Intermediates	For Advanced Skiers	For Children	Après-Ski	Other Sports	Value for Money
8	8	7	9	8	7	7	6	7

See also map p. 178–179.

THE RESORT

Straight off the Italian designer's drawing board, Sansicario is one of Europe's most attractive purpose-built resorts. Completed in 1973, it remains a cleverly structured, stylish collection of small apartment blocks, with a good selection of designer-fashion and sports shops. Just down the road is the original old village, equally appealing for its unspoiled character.

Well situated in the middle of the Milky Way chain, Sansicario offers challenging skiing possibilities for the intermediate and advanced skier.

THE SKIING

Defining the ski area is difficult. Very strictly speaking there are only 13 lifts and 38 km. of piste, but more realistically the immediate area is nearer 90 km. with 32 lifts, including neighbouring Cesana, Grangesises and Claviere. The views are good, too. Add to this the fact that just over the Fraiteve mountain are Sauze d'Oulx and Sestriere and in the other direction you can ski to Montgenèvre in France (snow permitting), and you come nearer to the Milky Way's full potential. This can be a challenge to intermediates and provides a great deal of off-piste for experts.

The one problem is that buying a lift pass for the whole lot has never been as simple as it ought to be, and the situation has deteriorated. The lack of a Milky Way pass is more of a problem for Sansicario residents than other linked resorts, as there is no pass which easily links neighbours Sestriere and Sauze d'Oulx, whilst the resorts that are included—Cesana and Claviere—are often separated skiwise by Cesana's low-altitude location. The excellent piste map offers some compensation by not only giving the ascent time of each lift but also a disclaimer, thoughtfully translated to loose English, stating that the piste management takes no responsibility for accidents occuring on certain vital Milky Way inter-resort links which it does not maintain.

Locally, Sansicario's lifts are laid out in such a way that it's only a short walk from, and you can usually ski back to, your accommodation. Nursery slopes are next to the village and there are a number of greens up at the Soleil Boeuf area. Intermediates and experts have a choice of reds or a black from Fraiteve, where the off-piste is usually good. Although a monorail lift links lower apartments with the main area, you may have a very short walk up to the lower lifts.

APRÈS-SKI

Comfortable and spacious modern bars are popular from close of lifts through to the small hours. The Drugstore crêperie/bar/pizzeria has photo-prints on the wall worth popping in to look at even if you don't want a drink. (If you do want a drink, make sure it's not a blizzard outside, as the toilets are in a subway across the square.)

There is a single disco, the Black Sun, complete with flashing dance floor, in the Hotel Sansicario. Other dancing is in the Hotel Rio Envers Gallia. The modern choice of restaurants in the resort may be complemented by more traditional fare down in the original village, a 20-minute walk away.

OTHER ACTIVITIES

A 10-km. cross country loop is available, plus all the variations of downhill skiing—monoski, snow-surf, parascending and heli-skiing. Although very much a skier's resort, there is an indoor swimming pool, sauna, fitness gym with weight-training, a darts board in the Fraiteve apartments, and indoor tennis courts elsewhere. There are plenty of browse-worthy shops, though prices are high. Otherwise Sansicario sadly cannot escape the normal "anti-atmosphere" feel that haunts all purpose-built resorts.

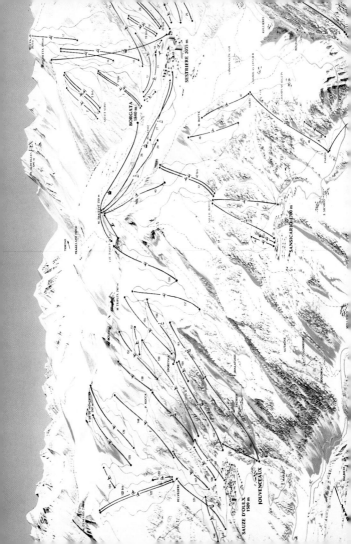

SANTA CATERINA

 +

Access: *Nearest airport:* Milan (4 hrs.). *By road:* N2 motorway to Como, then via Sondrio, Tirano. *By rail:* to Tirano, then by bus.
Tourist Office: I-23030 Santa Caterina Valfurva. Tel. (0342) 93 55 98

Altitude: 1738 m. *Top:* 2784 m.	Ski areas: Monte Sobretta
Language: Italian	Ski schools: Scuola di Sci Santa Caterina Valfurva
Beds: 1,800	
Population: 400	Linked resorts: None
Health: Doctor in resort. *Hospital:* Bormio (13 km.)	Season: December to April
	Kindergarten: *Non-ski:* none. *With ski:* None, but ski school from 5 years
Runs: 40 km.	
Lifts: 8	

Prices: *Lift pass:* 6 days L. 85,000–120,000 (children L. 60,000–85,000). *Ski school:* Group L. 45,000–70,000 for 6 half-days; private L. 25,000–28,000 per hour.

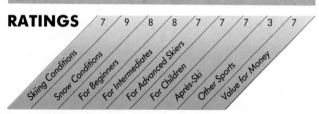

RATINGS

Skiing Conditions	Snow Conditions	For Beginners	For Intermediates	For Advanced Skiers	For Children	Après-Ski	Other Sports	Value for Money
7	9	8	8	7	7	7	3	7

THE RESORT

Dominated by the Tresero mountain, with thickly wooded lower slopes, Santa Caterina is in the Valfurva valley, not far from the Swiss border. It's also at the edge of the Stelvio National Park which helps to maintain the area's natural assets. The resort itself is small and not too exciting architecturally; but the residents have a reputation for friendliness and the village is often lively.

THE SKIING

Santa Caterina had a brief spell of international fame when it hosted the women's downhill race during the 1985 World Cup based in nearby Bormio (13 km.). The resort offers a reasonably priced lift pass which also covers Bormio, together with rather more distant duty-free Livigno.

More advanced skiers will quickly tire of Santa Caterina's two blacks, but are able to find more variety (if nothing more difficult) in Bormio. On the other hand, Santa Caterina's altitude usually gives it better snow conditions than its ''big brother'' so is often a better bet in times of general snow shortage—when Bormio's skiers head in the other direction. Good skiers will find Livigno's supermarket prices much more exciting than its pistes.

Back in Santa Caterina, the north-facing slopes are grouped together on the lower half of Monte Sobretta (3296 m.). The main lift out of town is the Paradiso chair (the rest of the eight lifts are drags) to Rif Paradiso. Altitude nursery slopes are served by three short drags and benefit from good snow conditions. The problem for total beginners is that the runs back to Santa Caterina are all intermediate. The problem is usually solved by taking the closed mountain pass road back, which should be well snow-covered, too.

Most of the skiing is intermediate standard. Drags go as far as Cresta Sobretta (2725 m.), from where reds and blacks descend to a middle lift or back to the village. Advanced skiers and good intermediates should enjoy the 3½-km. black Bucaneve run from the top station to the resort. Its vertical drop is 950 m., the bottom section through trees.

APRÈS-SKI

Despite its small size, Santa Caterina manages to maintain a lively après-ski atmosphere, spurred on by numerous hotel cellar discotheques. Those tempted to experience the greater scope of off-the-mountain and/or evening activities in Bormio should note that the last bus returns at 6 p.m., so you need your own transport or a taxi.

There is quite a lot going on in Santa Caterina itself, though. The recently constructed Ciao complex contains discotheque, video bar, pizzeria, piano bar, burger bar and has live music every night. There are additional discotheques at the hotels Alle Tre Baite, Park, Compagnoni and Sobretta. Eating out is normally in hotels, though there is one pizzeria.

OTHER ACTIVITIES

There are up to 30 km. of cross-country trails in the pine forest by the resort, as well as a floodlit natural ice rink, cleared paths, toboggans for hire, horse riding and sleigh-rides. A shopping (if not skiing) trip to Bormio is essential, of course, and excursions are normally organized to Lake Como, Livigno and St. Moritz.

SANTA CRISTINA

Access: *Nearest airport:* Milan (3 hrs.). *By road:* A22 motorway, exit Chiusa. *By rail:* to Bolzano/Bozen or Chiusa, then by bus.
Tourist Office: I-39047 Santa Cristina. Tel. (0471) 73 04 6

Altitude: 1428 m. *Top:* 2498 m.	Ski areas: Monte Pana, Col Raiser-Fermeda-Seceda, Sochers-Ciampinoi
Language: Italian, German, Ladin	
Beds: 2,935	Ski schools: Scuola di Sci Santa Cristina
Population: 1,598	
Health: Doctors in resort. *Hospital:* Bressanone/Brixen (35 km.)	Linked resorts: Arabba, Campitello, Canazei, Colfosco, Corvara, San Cassiano, Ortisei, Selva, La Villa
Runs: 50 km. (175 km. in Val Gardena)	Season: December to April
Lifts: 17 (85 in Val Gardena)	Kindergarten: *Non-ski:* none. *With ski:* none, but ski school from 4 years

Prices: *Lift pass:* 6 days L. 122,300–147,100. *Ski school:* Group L. 100,000 for 6 half-days; private L. 27,000 per hour.

RATINGS

Skiing Conditions	Snow Conditions	For Beginners	For Intermediates	For Advanced Skiers	For Children	Apres-Ski	Other Sports	Value for Money
8	8	7	9	8	7	6	2	7

See also map p. 14–15.

THE RESORT

Situated midway between Selva and Ortisei, Santa Cristina is in the centre of Val Gardena's skiing, and shares other benefits of the two larger resorts. The only one of the three to maintain its Austrian title after the Italians claimed the area following World War I, it's a loosely spaced, but attractive village, spreading out across a gentle hillside.

THE SKIING

The famous Val Gardena men's downhill run is in fact above Santa Cristina, though Selva is the resort most commonly associated with it. The main lift out of the village is a cable car, followed by a chair up to Ciampinoi (2250 m.) above the tree line and above Selva. Apart from it being the link route to the Sella Pass, you have the option of reds and blacks down through the trees to Selva or back to Santa Cristina. If you stay on Ciampinoi, you'll find mainly blues and reds, or you can go down to the small settlement of Plan de Gralba above Selva and take a long easy run back along the road.

Another option from Santa Cristina is a télécabine to Monte Pana, which is the main nursery area. A natural amphitheatre-shaped snow bowl is served by five short drags fanning out through 180°. It's a good sun trap and, as there's a tiny village here too, there are a few watering holes to make sure you're fully refreshed during those early days.

The other eight-man gondola from Santa Cristina departs from a kilometre or so out of town at Pramauron. This goes up to the Col Raiser and then on to Seceda above Ortisei. It's possible to ski down to Ortisei, but make sure you avoid the cliff, which can be seen more clearly from the two-stage cable cars back out of Ortisei to Seceda. There's a very pleasant long blue down from here all the way back to Santa Cristina, which makes the excursion worthwhile.

NT DE SEURA m 2117

SALTARIA

71

70

65

66

59

23

24

28   27

26

25

MONTE PANA

15

S. CRISTINA
m. 1446

S. GIACOMO
ST. JAKOB

CUCA

9

If you've purchased a Dolomiti Superski pass rather than the local Val Gardena one, you'll be able to go "over the top" at Danterceppies or the Passo Sella and join the Sella Ronda, an excellent circular route of more than 40 km. around the table-shaped Sella massif, taking in resorts such as Corvara, Colfosco and Arabba (as well as giving ski access to La Villa and the free coach up the Fassa Valley). Most of the skiing is easy intermediate standard, so it's fun for just about everyone. Since it's a slow-moving route, allow wide margins for catching the return lifts. A ski bus links all the Val Gardena resorts.

APRÈS-SKI

Although Santa Cristina is a small, quiet resort between two larger ones, it is friendly and relaxed. A few bars and restaurants are complemented by one discotheque, La Folta. There's also a dance hall—the Plaza, open several evenings a week and for tea dances between 5 and 7 p.m.

OTHER ACTIVITIES

There are several substantial cross-country loops along the valley, with a 10-km. one in Valunga Langental near Selva, and nearly 50 km. in total around Alpe di Siusi above Ortisei. In addition, there is monoski and toboggan hire.

Noteworthy places to visit in the area include the Chiesa di Santa Cristina, the bell tower of which dates back to 1342; and the Chiesa di San Giacomo, the oldest in the valley, built in the second half of the 12th century and boasting Gothic and Baroque frescoes.

SAN VIGILIO

Access: *Nearest airport:* Munich (3½ hrs.). *By road:* A22 motorway, exit Bressanone/Brixen. *By rail:* to Brunico/Bruneck, then by bus.

Tourist Office: I-39030 San Vigilio di Marebbe. Tel. (0474) 51 03 7

Altitude: 1201 m. *Top:* 2275 m.	Ski areas: Piz de Plaies, Plan de Corones
Language: Italian	
Beds: 3,500	Ski schools: Scuola di Sci San Vigilio di Marebbe
Population: 2,413	
Health: Doctors and dentist in resort. *Hospital:* Brunico/Bruneck (18 km.)	Linked resorts: Valdaora, Riscone
	Season: Mid-December to beginning April
Runs: 70 km.	
Lifts: 35	Kindergarten: *Non-ski:* from 3 years. *With ski:* from 3 years.

Prices: *Lift pass:* 6 days L. 113,000-150,000 (children 30–50 % reductions). *Ski school:* Group L. 105,000 for 6 half-days; private L. 27,000 per hour.

RATINGS

Skiing Conditions	Snow Conditions	For Beginners	For Intermediates	For Advanced Skiers	For Children	Après-Ski	Other Sports	Value for Money
8	8	9	8	5	7	8	7	7

See also map p. 14–15.

TOFANA　　　　　FANES　　　　　MARMOLADA

FANES H.　　　　RIF. LAVARELLA H.

CAMPILL
LONGIARÙ

CORVARA - GARDENA

S. VIGILIO
DI MAREBBE - ENNEBERG m 1201

PIZ DE PLAIES

ST. MARTIN i. T.
S. MARTINO i. B.

CURT

PEZES　　PIEVE ENNEBERG m 1284

LONGEGA
ZWISCHENWASSER

WELSCHELLEN
RINA

ONACH
ONIES

HORSCHWANG

STEFANSDORF
S. STEFANO

MAREBBE
ENNEBERG

MONTAL
MANTANA

ST. LORENZEN m 813
S. LORENZO DI SEBATO

EHRENBURG
CASTELDARNE

KIENS m 835
CHIENES

LINWALDEN　　PFALZEN
FALZES m 1022

ISSING
ISSENGO

MÜHLEN

HOFERN
CORTI

ST. SIGMUND
S. SIGISMONDO

© copyright by **cormar** bolzano

THE RESORT

Under Austrian rule until the start of the century, San Vigilio is a pretty village in chalet style. Part of the local Plan de Corones area and the larger Southern Tyrol region, it participates in the "Dolomiti Superski" lift-pass scheme. It's a good resort for children, with a popular "snow nursery" and a generally relaxed atmosphere across the resort.

THE SKIING

Skiing is possible on the eastern and western sides of the Marebbe Valley in which San Vigilio lies. The main area is around the Plan de Corones, linked by chair lift to the resort, and on the opposite side connected to neighbouring Valdaora.

A third resort sharing the mountain is Riscone which has a chair lift and cable car ascending from it. From here numerous pistes, largely of intermediate standard, radiate out, many with mountain huts and restaurants to serve the thirsty skier.

From Plan de Corones it's possible to go on up to Piz de Peres, which offers more intermediate skiing. Very advanced skiers may have a tough time finding challenging descents, but the steep run down to Riscone through the woods is not for the nervous.

The smaller Piz de Plaies ski area is across the valley, where drags serve the gentle village-side nursery slopes. With the pine trees around and mountain peaks in the distance, it's a beautiful spot to learn. A chair lift and télécabine lead to higher, intermediate runs.

Snow-making ensures good conditions throughout the season, and the ski bus is free with your visitor's card.

APRÈS-SKI

The village may be small, but nights are normally lively, with plenty of bars and restaurants from which to choose. Prices are generally good. The food influences come from both north and south, with the Hotel Condor serving excellent pizza, whilst the Speckstube caters for the Austrian palate. There is a discotheque in the Hotel Call, with alternatives such as the Club le Morin or frequent live music at the Hotel des Alpes.

OTHER ACTIVITIES

Cross-country skiers are well catered for with five trails ranging from 4 to 25 km. in length. There is an open-air (end of season) and large indoor pool; a sports hall with tennis, body-building, aerobics, sauna, solarium, massage and hot whirlpool; and a natural ice rink. Alternatives include pony trekking, an excellent toboggan run (with its own lift), and snow-boarding.

There are excursions to Bolzano, Cortina, Corvara and Innsbruck, and a tour of the Dolomites is organized from here.

SAUZE D'OULX

Access: *Nearest airport:* Turin (2 hrs.). *By road:* Fréjus Tunnel, then via Bardonecchia. *By rail:* to Oulx, then by bus.

Tourist Office: I-10050 Sauze d'Oulx. Tel. (0122) 85 00 9

Altitude: 1509 m. *Top:* 2507 m.	Ski areas: Clotes, Pian del Sole, Sportinia
Language: Italian	Ski Schools: Scuola di Sci Sauze d'Oulx, Scuola di Sci Sauze-Sportinia
Beds: 17,000	
Population: 800	
Health: Doctor in resort. *Hospital:* Susa (30 km.)	Linked resorts: Sestriere, Sansicario
Runs: 100 km. (250 with Sestriere)	Season: December to April
	Kindergarten: *Non-ski:* 6 months–6 years. *With ski:* from 3½ years
Lifts: 26 (50 with Sestriere)	

Prices: *Lift pass:* 6 days L. 125,000-145,000. *Ski school:* Group L. 100,000 for 6 half-days; private L. 23,000 per hour.

RATINGS

Skiing Conditions	Snow Conditions	For Beginners	For Intermediates	For Advanced Skiers	For Children	Après-Ski	Other Sports	Value for Money
7	7	6	8	6	4	8	4	6

For map see pp. 147 and 178–179.

THE RESORT

One of the few Italian resorts that unashamedly caters largely for foreign tourists (particularly British), Sauze d'Oulx is an excellent place if you like a lively nightlife. If you don't, it isn't a very excellent place at all.

If you want your ski resort to recreate a city-centre style collection of bars complete with video games and draught beer, with plenty of discos to follow, ''Sowzee Do'' wins hands down. It also offers good value for money, but the cheapness of the hotels here has been seriously let down as an overall package by a

sudden rise to the astronomical in lift pass prices, which (unless concessions are negotiated for you by your tour operator) must represent the worst value in the Alps.

The village itself has a large centre, but hotels and especially apartments are sometimes out on a limb, with a long uphill trudge back to some at the end of the day. Older parts of the resort are rustic and attractive, but these have been dwarfed by modern expansion. The residents here try to keep to themselves, tucked away in a corner and leaving the main street to the noisy tourists.

THE SKIING

The day begins in the queue for one of the closest chairs up to the Sportinia plateau. This is a favourite lunchtime meeting point, beginners' area and the junction of a large part of Sauze's skiing. From here the skiing branches out to more than 70 km. of piste, mainly through the trees. Red "motorways" abound—this is very much an intermediate resort.

Off-piste is good, particularly under the Rio Nero drag lift, with the network of runs always close at hand. Advanced skiers will find the descent from Monte Triplex (2507 m.) particularly exhilarating, with the odd mogul field to negotiate now and then. The runs over below Genevris and Moncrons are usually quieter than those surrounding Sportinia, offering all categories of descent.

Over the top into Sestriere is a daily experience, with good mountain restaurants dotted around at irregular intervals. A day's ski to Montgenèvre in France along with 300 km. of Milky Way skiing is also a must, although unfortunately a bus is usually needed for part of the trip.

Although sun conditions are normally good, snow conditions aren't so reliable, particularly at either end of the season.

The ski lifts are all at the top end of town and the linking buses, though running continuously, are not necessarily regular. The prices of the passes are amazingly high in peak season, but fall to about half in low season. Granted, the pass does cover the adjoining Sestriere region, which has new lifts and extensive snow-making.

APRÈS-SKI

Xenon's claims to be the most popular disco. Andy Capps, Moncro cocktail bar and the Hotel Derby's bar are popular watering holes with young Britons. More sophisticated nightlife is hard to find, but fancy dress parties, tobogganing evenings, "Miss Sauze" competitions and so on are frequently organized.

Practical problems are encountered by those wanting a good night out and a good night's sleep. Most of the hotels are situated in the centre of town, where the noise goes on till late. The quieter accommodation (including the apartments which make up four-fifths of it) is getting on for a kilometre away up the steep, slippery hill.

Eating out is no problem—there are numerous restaurants and pizzerias with high standards of cuisine (especially pizzas) and comparatively low prices. There's a cinema, but films are dubbed into Italian, unless you're very lucky.

OTHER ACTIVITIES

Sauze is a good resort for ski-bob, allowed on all the pistes, which are mainly served by drag lifts. Cross-country skiers have just a single 5-km. trail in Oulx, 5 km. away. Bowling, a sauna, two natural ice rinks and tobogganing complete the scene.

SELVA-WOLKENSTEIN

Access: *Nearest airport:* Milan (3 hrs.). *By road:* A22 motorway, exit Chiusa. *By rail:* to Bolzano/Bozen or Chiusa, then by bus.

Tourist Office: I-39048 Selva Gardena. Tel. (0471) 75 12 2

Altitude: 1563 m. *Top:* 2681 m.	Ski areas: Ciampinoi, Centro Paese, Danterceppies, Plan de Gralba, Passo Sella
Language: Italian, German, Ladin	Ski schools: Scuola Nazionale Italiana di Sci Selva Gardena
Beds: 5,000 in hotels, 3,000 in chalets and apartments	Linked resorts: Arabba, Campitello, Canazei, Colfosco, Corvara, San Cassiano, Santa Cristina, Ortisei, La Villa
Population: 2,300	
Health: Doctor in resort. *Hospital:* Bressanone/Brixen (35 km.)	Season: December to April
Runs: 175 km. in Val Gardena	Kindergarten: *Non-ski:* 4–12 years. *With ski:* 2–4 years
Lifts: 42 (85 in Val Gardena)	

Prices: *Lift pass:* 6 days L. 147,000 (children L. 103,000). *Ski school:* Group L. 95,000 for 14 hours per week; private L. 27,000 per hour.

RATINGS

Skiing Conditions	Snow Conditions	For Beginners	For Intermediates	For Advanced Skiers	For Children	Après-Ski	Other Sports	Value for Money
8	8	7	9	8	8	8	5	7

For map see p. 14–15 and 156–157.

THE RESORT

An Austrian village called Wolkenstein until after World War I, Selva is famous for its stunning Dolomite scenery, lively atmosphere, and for being host to the annual pre-Christmas FIS World Cup men's downhill race. More a small town than a village, it is rather attractively spread out in a higgledy-piggledy mixture of rustic old buildings and newer hotels. Skiing began here in the first decade of the century, prior to Italian rule. History is unusually rich for the area, with even an Oswald von Wolkenstein library open for limited hours each week. The locals maintain their own Ladin culture and language, together with a mixture of Austrian and German influences.

THE SKIING

Selva is well placed for the famous Val Gardena skiing and excursions to Alta Badia, as well as for skiing around the Sella Ronda which begins over the ridge and leads—eventually—to resorts like Arabba. It is not difficult skiing, but a lot of time-consuming lifts must be taken to do the circuit. Selva is one of the resorts where the Dolomiti Superski lift pass comes into its own.

Val Gardena's skiing has been criticized as not tough enough for experts. This may be true, but there are plenty of testing intermediate runs in Selva which are lacking in neighbouring resorts where the pistes are largely blue, with a couple of memorable blacks to make the reputation.

Above Selva there are numerous smooth cruises through thick woodland linking up with near neighbours Santa Cristina and Ortisei. The World Cup course (Sassolungho) is here, but not recommended for racers as it's invariably crowded.

Lifts ascend to the north, south and east. The main area for beginners is Danterceppies, also the access route to the Sella Ronda—its ridge overlooking Colfosco and Corvara—a beautiful long cruise away, nearly 10 km. in all. The nursery slopes are on a wide sunny plateau at the bottom of the mountain, but up above the village. A modern, efficient, six-man télécabine goes up the whole slope, and intermediates will find a number of long, angled, fast descents cutting down through the trees—even advanced skiers should find these entertaining at a higher speed.

From Ciampinoi on the south side, there are several steep runs back to Selva or Santa Cristina (including the World Cup course). There are numerous drags and chairs above here following in a vaguely southerly direction towards Canazei, the south-west corner of the Sella Ronda at the north-east end of the Fassa Valley.

The final area to the north is the scarcely used Seceda, mainly above Santa Cristina and Ortisei and best reached via them. The runs are generally blue or easy red standard here.

APRÈS-SKI

Selva is almost certainly the liveliest resort on the Sella Ronda circuit, with tea dances in two establishments after the lifts close, live music continuing throughout the evening in two, and a further five popular discotheques also open. The Stella bar, a roomy place in the centre of town, never stops buzzing. The Speckkeller is equally popular, particularly straight after skiing, though it keeps on going into the small hours. There are many other establishments, equally good, and plenty of good restaurants and pizzerias such as the Ciampinoi, which is also popular for lunches.

OTHER ACTIVITIES

Although there is only 15 km. of cross-country skiing in Selva itself, there are more than 50 km. of trails in the Val Gardena. The Hotel Gran Baita has a games room, sauna, solarium and large indoor pool open to the public. Hotel Antares has a pool, sauna and Jacuzzi. There's also bowling, indoor ice skating and curling, tennis and billiards.

SESTRIERE

Access: *Nearest airport:* Turin (2½ hrs.) *By road:* Grand St. Bernard Tunnel, then via Aosta. *By rail:* to Oulx, then by bus.
Tourist Office: I-10058 Sestriere. Tel. (0122) 76 04 5

Altitude: 2035 m. *Top:* 2823 m.	Ski schools: Scuola di Sci Sestriere, Scuola di Sci Borgata Sestriere, Scuola di Sci Grangesises
Language: Italian	
Beds: 14,000	
Population: 800	Linked resorts: Sauze d'Oulx, Sansicario, Jouvenceaux, Cesana, Claviere, Montgenèvre (France)
Health: Doctor and fracture clinic in resort. *Hospital:* Susa (46 km.)	
Runs: 120 km. (250 km. with Sauze d'Oulx)	Season: November to April
Lifts: 26	Kindergarten: *Non-ski:* none. *With ski:* none, but ski school from 4 years
Ski areas: Monte Fraiteve, Grangesises, Monte Sises, Monte Banchetta, Borgata	

Prices: *Lift pass:* 6 days L. 171,000. *Ski school:* Group L. 27,000 for 3 hours; private L. 27,000 per hour.

RATINGS

Skiing Conditions	Snow Conditions	For Beginners	For Intermediates	For Advanced Skiers	For Children	Après-Ski	Other Sports	Value for Money
8	8	5	8	8	5	8	6	8

For map see pp. 147 and 178–179.

THE RESORT

The world's first purpose-built ski resort (by Fiat in 1934) was treated then—as its French descendants are now—with a certain amount of distrust by the skiing fraternity, who hesitate to enjoy a holiday in a resort that cannot claim to have once been a charming little Alpine village. Sestriere was, until its creation, a piece of extremely barren mountain. It's not the most hospitable place on earth now, but the skiing is extensive and wide ranging, the après-ski likewise, and the prices are reasonable for what is a higher standard Italian resort.

THE SKIING

If you wanted a resort between three mountains, linked to several others on a famous ski circuit (the Milky Way) and with Europe's largest snow-making facility, then you'd be directed to Sestriere. The season is long, from November to April, and the lift pass also covers Sauze d'Oulx, though unfortunately there is still not a Milky Way pass as such.

Beginners will find nursery slopes well situated near the village, but should consider how much they'll use what is, for the first timer, an expensive lift pass. A well-designed and adequate lift system means that queues are rarely a problem, except at the odd holiday weekend.

Of the three mountains, Sises offers a number of lively descents for the advanced intermediate, and Banchetta has long intermediate runs and off-piste opportunities. Monte Fraiteve is the link with the other Milky Way resorts, though the route is sometimes short of snow. Its best feature is probably the resort's most famous run, the 8-km. Rio Nero.

APRÈS-SKI

Night times are normally lively but not loud. The "crowd" receives a boost at weekends and national holidays when the residents of Turin, for whom the resort was built, pour in. But there is more of an air of chic here than in the downmarket resorts. The Tabata discotheque normally fills first, but perhaps only because the Black Sun is so large. For the early evening there is a wide selection of good quality bars, pizzerias and restaurants. The resort also has a cinema.

OTHER ACTIVITIES

It's possible to manipulate your hotel/lift pass package to include ice driving. Club Colombiere has sauna, gymnasium and an open-air heated swimming pool, while the Palazzetto Sport has tennis, squash, basketball and a sauna. There's also a 2½-km. cross-country run in the resort, not to mention a kart track. Skating too is available, of course, and ski-jumping for the courageous.

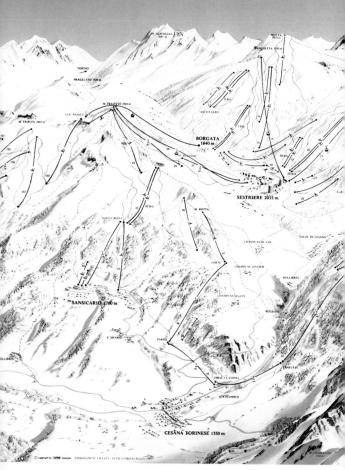

179

LA THUILE

Access: *Nearest airport:* Turin (2½ hrs.); Geneva (3 hrs.). *By road:* Mont. Blanc Tunnel, then via Pré-St-Didier. *By rail:* to Pré-St-Didier, then by bus.

Tourist Office: I-11016 La Thuile. Tel. (0165) 88 41 79

Altitude: 1450 m. *Top:* 2642 m.	Lifts: 16
Language: Italian, French	Ski areas: Les Suches, Chaz Dura, Belvedere
Beds: 882 in hotels, 1,096 in apartments	Ski schools: Scuola di Sci Rutor
Population: 730	Linked resorts: La Rosière (France)
Health: Medical and fracture clinic in resort. *Hospital:* Aosta (39 km.)	Season: December to April
Runs: 50 km.	Kindergarten: *Non-ski:* none. *With ski:* from 5 years

Prices: *Lift pass:* 6 days L. 111,000-129,000. *Ski school:* Group: L. 25,000 per day; private L. 20,000–40,000 per hour.

RATINGS

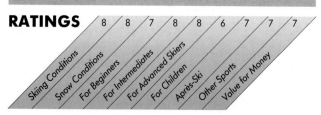

Skiing Conditions	Snow Conditions	For Beginners	For Intermediates	For Advanced Skiers	For Children	Après-Ski	Other Sports	Value for Money
8	8	7	8	8	6	7	7	7

THE RESORT

An interesting combination of old "abandoned" mining town, predictable semi-smart new ski developments and even a barracks for the Italian Army Corps, La Thuile is one of the few Italian resorts with a definite French connection which can be included on the lift pass. La Rosière extends the skiing area from 50 km. to more than 80 km. and doubles the number of lifts available. Those who want a picturesque setting have arguably the best Italian view of Mont Blanc from here, and the resort is dominated by the Rutor glacier.

THE SKIING

Of the five Aosta Valley resorts featured in this guide, La Thuile has the best range of skiing, with a series of excellent reds and blacks down through the trees from Les Suches. The first lift has been replaced by a new cable car "DMC", carrying 3,000 people per hour. It is unique in Italy and links La Thuile and Les Suches at 2200 m. Higher up, from Belvedere at 2642 m., above the tree line, numerous wide reds and blues descend back to La Thuile or over down to La Rosière. The run over the Petit St. Bernard (the same route in reverse probably taken by Hannibal and the elephants hundreds of years ago) is a long easy motorway, but the piste back includes a "short black", though a new link is soon to be forged. The black is in fact not very difficult and quite brief.

Snow conditions here have been good in recent years when other Aosta resorts have suffered "short falls". On the other hand, piste maintenance seems to be kept to a minimum, though signposting is good. For some, the lack of piste-bashing is an

asset, for others the ensuing ruts and bumps make the going too tough for their liking. The compensations include few queues.

Mountain-eating is best over in La Rosière, which is above Bourg-St-Maurice, across the valley from Les Arcs, if you plan to be really adventurous. On the Italian side, La Thuile is only 45 minutes from Courmayeur, so skiing day-trips are easy.

The old mining village of La Thuile has renewed its identity with smart, modern ski development.

APRÈS-SKI

A good complement of restaurants and pizzerias is the most La Thuile can boast of. Otherwise things tend to be quiet, especially in the old part and mid-week. The single discotheque, La Bricole, at the junction of the old and new parts of the village is worth a look in. It combines bar, restaurant and cellar disco in a well-converted old building.

OTHER ACTIVITIES

There is limited cross-country skiing with a 1-km. easy run, 3-km. and 5-km. medium loops and a 7½-km. difficult trail. Most sports other than skiing are concentrated in the Planibel complex and include indoor swimming pools and ice rink, good squash courts, sauna, massage, gym, bowling, basketball and other facilities. The ice rink has a lights-disco every night. Outside there's tobogganing.

TRAFOI

 +

Access: *Nearest airport:* Innsbruck (2 hrs.); Verona (3½ hrs.). *By road:* N2 motorway to Lugano, then via Sondrio and over Passo Stelvio. *By rail:* to Spondigna, then by bus.

Tourist Office: I-39020 Trafoi/Stelvio. Tel. (0473) 611 67 7

Altitude: 1600 m. *Top:* 2300 m.	Lifts: 6
Language: German, Italian	Ski areas: Forcola, Campo Piccolo, Belvedere
Beds: 430	
Population: 140	Ski schools: Scuola di Sci Trafoi
Health: Doctor in resort. *Hospital:* Silandro (30 km.)	Linked resorts: None
	Season: December to April
Runs: 10 km.	Kindergarten: None

Prices: *Lift pass:* 6 days L. 70,000 (children L. 45,000). *Ski school:* Group L. 48,000 for 6 half-days (children L. 42,000); private L. 25,000 per hour.

RATINGS

Skiing Conditions	Snow Conditions	For Beginners	For Intermediates	For Advanced Skiers	For Children	Après-Ski	Other Sports	Value for Money
8	9	8	6	3	7	5	1	7

THE RESORT

Trafoi is a small village at the foot of the Stelvio Valley near Bormio. The Ortler mountains here are, roughly speaking, at the centre of the Alps and are some of the highest. The resort lies in the South Tyrol, Austrian until World War I, and virtually all the buildings are typical large Tyrolean chalet style. It's a cosy, friendly little resort. Glaciers in the area allow for year-round skiing, though Trafoi is equally popular with cyclists in the summer months. The local hero is Gustav Thöni, Olympic and world (four times) skiing champion.

THE SKIING

With only one chair lift and five drags, Trafoi is the smallest resort to be featured in this guide. But it is also a good example of the vast majority of Italian resorts, where the novice or beginner can enjoy an excellent holiday without the distractions (and intimidation) of racing skiers endlessly using them as slalom poles. Another bonus is that you won't pay for the facilities of a vast lift

network of which you're only going to use a fraction. Where Trafoi differs from many of the small Italian resorts, is that it's at a reasonable height, and well organized for skiing.

The chair lift ascends from beside the Posthotel to the main station, Forcola (2300 m.), where there's a good restaurant. The ascent takes about 20 minutes through the woods and arrives just above the tree line. From here there's a choice of three lifts: two T-bars offering easy blue pistes, or a button drag to the top station (2700 m.) where the views of the Madatsch mountain (3313 m.) across the valley are excellent. From here there's a choice of two blackish runs back to the middle station, or all the way down to Trafoi. As you have ascended 1150 m. since getting on the chair at the bottom, you can imagine that both easy and medium descents back through the trees are quite lengthy and thoroughly enjoyable.

There are nursery slopes at the top of the village, which catch the sun for most of the day. If more advanced skiers (three weeks plus) do want to base themselves in Trafoi, an Ortler Skiarena lift pass covers several neighbouring resorts, the nearest being Solda, a 30-minute drive away. Getting about in ski boots whilst carrying skis, would be rather difficult without your own transport, however.

APRÈS-SKI

A small village cannot hope to have a vast selection of nightlife, but there are pleasant, friendly taverns-cum-discos/dance halls in the basement of the two main hotels, Posthotel and Madatsch. This is an ideal location if you want to spend a week or two getting to know your fellow guests and the village residents—you can't get away from one another! You could try a different hotel restaurant if you're not on half board.

OTHER ACTIVITIES

There's an indoor swimming pool, sauna and games room in both the hotels Posthotel and Madatsch. Tour operators usually offer excursions to duty-free Livigno (about an hour's drive), neighbouring Solda or across the border to St. Moritz in Switzerland.

LA VILLA

Access: *Nearest airport:* Innsbruck (2 hrs.), Venice (2 hrs.). *By road:* A22 motorway, exit Bressanone/Brixen, then via Brunico/Bruneck. *By rail:* to Brunico/Bruneck, then by bus.

Tourist Office: I-39030 La Villa Stern. Tel. (0471) 84 70 37

Altitude: 1433 m. *Top:* 2077 m.	Ski areas: Piz La Villa
Language: Italian	Ski schools: Scuola di Sci La Villa
Beds: 1,300	
Population: 790	Linked resorts: Arabba, Campitello, Canazei, Colfosco, Corvara, San Cassiano, Santa Cristina, Selva, Ortisei
Health: Doctors in Corvara and Pedraces. *Hospital:* Brunico/Bruneck (30 km.)	
	Season: December to Mid-April
Runs: 130 km. in Alta Badia	
Lifts: 8 (53 in Alta Badia)	Kindergarten: None

Prices: *Lift pass:* 6 days Alta Badia L. 147,000 (children L. 103,300). *Ski school:* Group L. 94,000–97,000 for 6 half-days; private L. 24,000 per hour.

RATINGS

Skiing Conditions	Snow Conditions	For Beginners	For Intermediates	For Advanced Skiers	For Children	Après-Ski	Other Sports	Value for Money
8	8	8	8	6	6	4	1	7

For map see pp. 14–15 and 62–63.

THE RESORT

Most of La Villa was purpose built two decades ago, but the resort is in no way similar to better-known compact multi-storey blocks elsewhere. On the contrary, the 20 or so hotels and pensions seem to be spread out as widely as possible along the Passo Falzarego road. Equally surprising, perhaps, it has been built at a lower altitude than the original village. Situated a few kilometres from Corvara and Colfosco to the south-west and San Cassiano to the south-east, La Villa has few facilities of its own and therefore shares them with neighbouring resorts in the Alta Badia region.

THE SKIING

The nursery slope by the village has its own mini drag, a nice gentle gradient and is separated from the main skiing. Beginners will also appreciate the longer drag nearby, which rises to 1760 m. and serves two pleasant blue runs.

The principal lift, a cable car, takes you to Piz La Villa (2077 m.) from where the return red or black runs cut through the trees are very good (the black is a World Championship downhill course). Both have snow-making facilities and a vertical drop of more than 600 m. in their 5/6 km. lengths.

Piz La Villa is also the start of a large ski area, shared with San Cassiano and Corvara, up above the tree line. The runs here are mainly blue, served by drags, with a peak (Pralongià) at 2140 m. Much of the remaining area, however, is also above 2000 m., so the vertical drop is small.

Although essentially an access area to Corvara and the Sella Ronda, it is not too well signposted. Red runs drop back down to Corvara and San Cassiano, though both are also served by long blues all the way down from Pralongià.

Across Corvara's main street, lifts link into the Sella Ronda circuit, giving easy ski access to Selva, Ortisei and Arabba, all covered by the Dolomiti Superski pass. It's a full-day excursion from La Villa over to Corvara and then "round the Ronda" to one of these resorts. Be very careful with timings if you try it.

APRÈS-SKI

This is mostly limited to hotel bars, which can be lively. The Aurora Hotel, near the main lift in the village centre, is particularly popular and has a spacious basement nightclub, usually with live band. This is La Villa's only real nightspot, though there is also a bar at the nearby Dolomiti Hotel. There is more late-night entertainment in neighbouring San Cassiano (3 km.) and at a few of the hotels along the road between. Corvara (4 km. away) has plenty of discotheques for those looking for a merry time. Stay in La Villa if you prefer a bit of peace. You might enjoy a sleigh-ride, and there's more laid on during the annual carnival.

OTHER ACTIVITIES

There is curling, swimming, ice-skating, bowling (hotels Dolasilla, Dolomiti and La Villa) and cleared winter paths. If you do venture to San Cassiano, you'll find five hotels with indoor pools (though rarely open to the public), and the Hotel Diamant there has indoor tennis and two bowling alleys. Cross-country skiing is possible in the valley, conditions permitting.

BERLITZ SKI-INFO

An A-Z Summary of Practical Information, Facts and Advice

CONTENTS

A ACCOMMODATION

Hotels. Italy's hotels are divided into five categories, with a one- to five-star rating to guide you. Most European countries have a number of booking agencies which arrange hotel accommodation in Italy in advance. Details can be obtained from the Italian National Tourist Office (ENIT), but you can't make reservations through them.

Hotel rates are fixed according to the number of stars. Make sure that the price quoted is *tutto compreso* ("all inclusive")—otherwise up to 20% can be added to your bill in the form of service charges, tourist tax and VAT (IVA). You are required by Italian law to keep an official receipt.

Pensioni are small family-style boarding houses, often with more character and a homelier atmosphere than hotels; but they will offer fewer facilities and may not have a restaurant.

Chalets. Chalet-style holidays are not common in Italy, though some tour operators offer them in the more traditionally stylish resorts such as Courmayeur and Cortina d'Ampezzo.

Apartments. Increasingly popular in modern Italian ski resorts, apartment holidays can offer a cheap alternative to hotels or *pensioni*. Unlike in other purpose-built European resorts—where blocks of hundreds of apartments cramming as many people as possible into a minimal space are the rule—Italian apartments are dispersed among numerous small buildings and tend to be more spacious and individual, owned by families rather than companies.

Mountain huts (*rifugi alpini*). There are more than 500 mountain huts which offer overnight accommodation for a small fee. Comforts are, of course, basic. The Club Alpino Italiano will supply a list of the huts with their telephone numbers. The address is: 3, Via Ugo Foscolo, 20121 Milan; tel. (02) 869 2584

AIRPORTS

Italian ski resorts are dispersed through the northern part of the country from above the French to the Yugoslavian border. It is fair to say that the majority of Italian resorts are

not the easiest in Europe to reach by air, and often flights to **A**
airports in France, Switzerland or Austria are preferred.
Within Italy, the Aosta Valley resorts and central northern
Italy are served by Turin, but operators often prefer Zurich
for far northern resorts like Livigno, and Innsbruck for the
South Tyrol and Dolomites. Venice, Verona, Geneva and
Grenoble are other possibilities. However, your two most
likely destinations remain:

Milan. Linate airport, situated 7 km. east of the city centre.
There is a regular bus service to the centre of Milan, from
where the public buses serving the ski resorts leave.
Transfer by train from the city centre is also possible. An
ENIT tourist information office operates in the airport and can
help with enquiries.

Turin. Caselle airport, situated about 15 km. from the centre
of town, from where you can pick up a connecting bus to your
chosen resort. Transfer by train from the city centre is also
possible.

BOOKING (See also INSURANCE.) **B**

The market leaders in the ski tour-operator business are still
best booked through a travel agent, but for some smaller
operators you may have to book direct. Wading through
tour-operator brochures can sometimes be more confusing
than helpful, until you know exactly what to look for, though
even the most experienced sometimes find they haven't got
what they want. Books exist solely on the subject of finding
the right holiday to suit your needs and budget. Another idea
is to look through the specialist magazines, especially
around September and October, as they usually carry out
detailed analyses of what's on offer.

If you are booking through a tour operator, air transport
and transfer by coach to your resort are included in the cost
of your holiday. Some will even offer you free or discounted
travel from your home to your departure airport, especially
if there is a group booking. These companies get very good
flight deals, so if you make your own way but take their
accommodation, you won't find you've made much of a

B saving. Some operators offer a coach alternative—cheaper, but also long and tiring.

Package tours cater for everyone—from all-inclusive learn-to-ski weeks (travel, accommodation, lift pass, equipment hire, tuition) to advanced off-piste powder weeks. Book with one of the giants for competitive prices in hotels or self-catering. Go through a specialist company for something different and personal service.

Many companies offer early-booking and full payment discounts (brochures come out already in summer) and most one free place in every ten bookings, and discounts for children. Most companies now offer a snow guarantee whereby they transport you free of charge to a nearby resort with snow or refund you for every ski day lost. Read the small print at the end of the brochure and make sure you will get a full refund should the company cancel your trip, as well as fair refund if you have to back out; percentage refunds decrease the closer cancellation is to departure date. The tendency is for larger operators to give a better deal than the smaller ones.

Other interesting features in the brochures are special January reductions and free airport car parking. A few companies cater for long weekends and 10/11 night options and others offer gourmet chalet or luxury hotel accommodation.

You can, of course, arrange your holiday independently, but it works out cheaper in the long run to travel package.

One possibility, if you are travelling independently: most of the Italian winter sports resorts offer *settimane bianche* or ''white weeks'', from the end of November until April. These are special packages which include accommodation, ski lessons and lift passes. Information should be obtained directly from the tourist office of the ski resort in which you are interested.

C CHILDREN

More and more parents are taking even tiny babies on skiing holidays. The modern idea is that the sooner the child is introduced to the snow environment the better, it being allowed to ''grow up'' on skis.

196

Several tour companies have recognized this market potential and provide English nannies, though these are still rare for Italy. Many others have family accommodation, nanny weeks and, occasionally, crèche facilities. There is a great range of reductions for children, so look out for good deals—even free places.

Many resorts in Italy suffer from limited provision for children. Kindergartens are rare, discounts for children on lifts and ski school likewise, and English-speaking staff where such facilities do exist are hard to find. It's usually best to rely on what a tour operator can offer.

Obviously children, particularly babies, will feel the cold, so do take adequate clothing. All-in-one padded suits are best, with a vest and a couple of lightweight jumpers underneath, mittens (attached to the suit or they'll disappear) and always a hat (preferably tied on) or, better still, a hood which insulates the ears well. Sensitive eyes and skin must be well protected. Ordinary sunglasses will not do. Invest in a pair with 100 per cent UV (ultra-violet) and IR (infra-red) block. Use extra-high-protection sun block (Factor 15). Cold air dries the skin; ask your chemist for a suitable cream to prevent this.

Take with you any specialist items—food, toiletries, etc—which may be hard to find abroad.

CLIMATE

The mountain climate in northern Italy is extremely changeable. The higher the resort, the colder it will be, but the sun will be strong when it's out. North-facing slopes will obviously be colder than south-facing ones because they don't get the sun. Remember the wind-chill factor (especially if skiing at speed).

Recent Decembers have been warm and sunny, but disappointing with regard to snow cover. Watch out for frostbite in January and February (see HEALTH AND MEDICAL CARE), especially at the top of the mountain; it can be pleasant at resort level and a raging blizzard on high. March and April can be gloriously hot and sunny. Good snow lasts into April at higher resorts. Lower ones tend to get patchy in late March, south-facing slopes become slushy by midday and it

C has been known to rain! When it rains in the resort, it's snowing higher up the mountain, so all is not lost.

While skiing, you are often in the clouds. If it is foggy in the village, don't despair. You may well climb way above it to sunny slopes and look down on a sea of mist. Conversely, sometimes it's better to stick to lower slopes because the peak is in cloud.

The snow never melts in high glacial mountain areas, but summer weather can be equally deceptive. A sunny shirts-off day can deteriorate rapidly into arctic conditions. Remember it is much colder on the glacier than in the village below.

The resort tourist office usually pins the weather forecast outside for skiers to consult.

A recorded bulletin on general weather conditions (in Italian) can be obtained by phoning (06) 592 5998. The Automobile Club d'Italia (ACI) will also give information on weather and snow conditions (see DRIVING).

CLOTHING AND ACCESSORIES

Be prepared! Due to the vagaries of mountain weather (see CLIMATE) always err on the cautious side. It's better to sweat a bit than die of hypothermia. The outer ski suit can be a one-piece or ski pants (stretchy racing ones or padded salopettes) and a jacket. The advantage of the former is that snow can't get up your back and it's comfortable to wear. Choose a two-piece if you want the jacket to double as après-ski wear or even casual gear back home. The jacket will ideally have a high collar, incorporating a roll-up hood, and close-fitting cuffs. Look closely at the label: Gore-Tex, Entrant and Cyclone are waterproof; Thinsulate and Isodry supply lightweight warmth; Tactel is ICI's great, new waterproof fibre ideal for ski wear.

Several thin layers under your suit provide better insulation than a bulky jersey. Natural fibres—silk, cotton, wool—wick moisture away from the skin. A long-sleeved thermal vest and long johns are essential, with a cotton skiing roll-neck and possibly another thin woollen jumper or a sweatshirt. It really depends on the thermal qualities of your suit, the weather and individual needs. If too hot, you can

always take a layer off and tie it round your waist. It helps to **C**
carry a rucksack or bumbag to house accessories. You only
need to wear one pair of tube-type ski socks (not ribbed).

Mitts are warmer than gloves, but you have to take them off
to adjust boots and bindings. Either get leather handwear or
Gore-Tex. Carry a pair of silk glove-liners and a silk
balaclava just in case—frostbite sets in very quickly. A large
percentage of body heat is lost through the head, so have a
hat with you always. Headbands are good, too, for keeping
the ears cosy.

Goggles and specs are most important. Always take both
with you whatever the weather in the valley. A yellow-amber
tint gives best definition. Never economize on eyewear.
Altitude and reflection off the snow increase damage to the
cornea caused by ultra-violet radiation. Make sure the lenses
block out damaging UV—and infra-red if possible. Dark
lenses that do not block out ultra-violet rays are more
dangerous because the pupil dilates, allowing more rays in.

Although ski wear has become a fashion commodity,
practicality should take precedence over colour and style.

Après-ski. Take loose and comfortable clothes to change
into for the evening after the rigours of a day's labours on the
slopes. Few hotels observe formal dining requirements, but
it's a good idea for men to take a tie in case circumstances
demand. Dancing in après-ski boots is difficult, so if you visit
a local discotheque, it's not a bad idea to have a pair of
lightweight shoes or slippers tucked into your pocket or
bag.

DRIVING   **D**

Entering Italy. To take your car into Italy you will need:

- International Driving Permit or your national driving
  licence
- car registration papers
- Green Card (an extension to your regular insurance
  policy, making it valid specifically for Italy)
- nationality plate or sticker
- red warning triangle in case of breakdown
- a set of spare bulbs

D In Italy it is compulsory to have a left-hand wing mirror. In order not to dazzle oncoming traffic at night, you can buy special black tape to mask a portion of the left-hand side of the headlights. These stickers come in sizes to suit your car model and are obtainable from local dealers.

Naturally, you should ensure your car is in excellent working order and likely to stand up to the extreme conditions encountered in mountain driving and parking. If your car engine is water cooled, make sure you have a good anti-freeze, and a strong solution for the windscreen wash. A tow rope and shovel are recommended.

Foreign motorists may purchase coupons from certain banks, travel agents and automobile clubs and from border offices of the Automobile Club d'Italia (ACI) entitling them to discounts on petrol, motorway toll charges and breakdown services. Ask your travel agent or motoring organization for the latest regulations, as these are always changing.

Driving regulations. The numerous rules for driving abroad should be checked with your insurance company or motoring organization. As elsewhere on the continent, drive on the right, overtake on the left. Traffic on major roads has right of way over that entering from side roads and at intersections cars coming from the right theoretically have priority, but this is frequently ignored, so be very careful.

Speed limits. In Italy, these are based on the car engine size. The following chart gives the engine size in cubic centimetres and the limits (in kilometres per hour) on the open road. The limit in built-up areas is usually 50 kph.

Engine size	less than 600 cc.	600 to 900 cc.	900 to 1300 cc. (and motor-cycles more than 150 cc.)	more than 1300 cc.
Main roads Motorways (Express-ways	80 kph 90 kph	90 kph 110 kph	100 kph 130 kph	110 kph 140 kph

Motoring organizations. The Italian Automobile Club **D**
(Automobile Club d'Italia—ACI) has its headquarters at
5, Via Magenta, 00185 Rome, tel: (06) 42 12. Here, drivers can
obtain traffic information, weather reports, addresses of
garages, urgent personal messages and so on.

In Britain consult the Automobile Association (AA), Fanum
House, Basingstoke, Hants., tel: (0256) 20123; or the Royal
Automobile Club (RAC), P.O. Box 100, RAC House, Lans-
downe Road, Croydon, Surrey, tel: (01) 686 2525.

The AA and RAC both produce excellent booklets, *Guide
to Motoring Abroad* and *Continental Motoring Guide*. The
latter has a section on toll roads and mountain passes. Both
also have insurance schemes for members and non-mem-
bers. Obtain your Green Card through the AA.

Road conditions. In Italy, motorways *(autostrada)* generally
have two lanes, with service stations at least every 25 km. A
toll is payable at the end of each section depending on axle
ratio, vehicle length and distance travelled. Charges are
higher on mountain motorways than elsewhere. (If passing
through Switzerland, you must display a toll disc on your
windscreen, obtainable at the border upon entry or from
your home motoring organization; Austria and France have
toll gates at strategic intervals.)

It is cheaper, but time-consuming and a lot less convenient
to take alternative toll-free roads. In Italy, these are known as
superstrada (high-speed clearways) and *strada statale*
(trunk roads). In the mountains, such roads are much less
likely to be passable.

Breakdowns. There are emergency telephones every
2 km. on the *autostrade*, with instructions for use in Italian,
English, French and German. Switch on the flashing warning
lights and place a warning triangle 50 metres behind your
car (greater distance on the motorway). You can dial 116 for
breakdown service from the ACI. It's wise to have internationally valid breakdown insurance, and to ask for an
estimate (with VAT added) *before* undertaking repairs.

Fuel and oil. Service stations abound in Italy, most with at
least one mechanic on duty (who's likely to be a Fiat
specialist). Most stations close on Sundays, and every day

D from noon to 3 p.m. Fuel sold at government-set prices, comes in super (98–100 octane), unleaded (95 octane)—still rare—and normal (86–88 octane).

Mountain roads. Extra care should be taken on mountain roads, which in addition to being steep and with continuous hairpin bends, are often potholed and icy.

There is a special art to driving on ice and in snowy conditions. The golden rule is always to drive more slowly than you think you should. Avoid sharp reactions or sudden braking; it's better to anticipate well in advance, such as keeping a good distance from the car in front (two or three times the normal braking distance). When starting off or going uphill, put the car in the highest possible gear to avoid wheel spin. Never drive in ski or après-ski boots.

Alpine passes. Many passes close during winter months, often for six months or more. However, the following routes are normally kept open by snow plough:

Bracco (Italy), Brenner (Austria–Italy), Fugazze (Italy), Mauria (Italy), Mendola (Italy), Monte Croce di Comelico (Italy), Montgenèvre (France–Italy), Resia (Austria–Italy), Sestriere (Italy), Tenda (Italy–France) and Tonale (Italy).

Tunnels are often quicker than going over a pass (if the queue isn't too long), but more often than not you will have to pay a toll. The tunnel linking St. Moritz and Livigno is remarkable in that it is extremely long, bent in the middle (where the Swiss and Italian engineers met), is very smooth at the Swiss end, rough hewn at the Italian end and is said to have Swiss explosives built into the walls so that it can be destroyed in the event of war. It also tends to close overnight.

Parking. Italian ski resorts are hardly ever car-free and sometimes there are cars to excess. Try to park your car in a place where it, or at least the engine, will be sheltered from the wind and the handbrake can be left off (to avoid it being frozen on). But then don't forget to leave the car in gear! Pull windscreen wipers away from the glass.

Roofracks. Skiing luggage, if you have all the equipment, can be excessive. Boxes which fit onto the roof are excellent (though expensive) and protect skis and other belongings from the elements. Regular ski roofracks cost less and can **D** also be hired from some ski hire shops or the AA (Dover branch only).

Winter tyres and snow chains. You can get your car fitted with winter tyres which grip better than regular tyres, but even these may not be good enough for some snowy mountain roads. Studded tyres are subject to restrictions: there is a speed limit of 90 kph; they can only be used from 15 November to 15 March; and only on vehicles weighing less than 3,500 kg.

On many mountain roads it is obligatory to have chains in the car even if conditions do not necessitate their use. These come in various tyre sizes and vary in price usually according to sophistication and ease of handling. Major ski shops hire them out, as do the AA (Dover branch). Practise putting on your chains *before* you get stuck in heavy snow.

ENTRY REQUIREMENTS   E

For a stay of up to three months, a valid passport is sufficient for most citizens of western European countries. Visitors from the United Kingdom and Eire need only an identity card to enter Italy.

Here are some main items you can take into Italy duty-free and, when returning home, into your own country:

Entering	Cigarettes		Cigars		Tobacco	Spirits		Wine
Italy from: 1)	200	or	50	or	250 g.	¾ l.	or	2 l.
2)	300	or	75	or	400 g.	1.5 l.	and	3 l.
3)	400	or	100	or	500 g.	¾ l.	or	2 l.
Into:								
Australia	200	or	250 g.	or	250 g.	1 l.	or	1 l.
Canada	200	and	50	and	900 g.	1 l.	or	1 l.
Eire	200	or	50	or	250 g.	1 l.	and	2 l.
N. Zealand	200	or	50	or	250 g.	1.1 l.	and	4.5 l.
S. Africa	400	and	50	and	250 g.	1 l.	and	2 l.
U.K.	200	or	50	or	250 g.	1 l.	and	2 l.
U.S.A.	200	and	100	and	4)	1 l.	or	1 l.
1) non-EEC countries within Europe 3) countries outside Europe								
2) EEC countries 4) a reasonable quantity								

E Currency restrictions. Non-residents may import or export up to L. 500,000 in local currency. In foreign currencies, you may import unlimited amounts, but to take the equivalent of more than L. 5,000,000 in or out of the country, you must fill out a V2 declaration form at the border upon entry.

EQUIPMENT (See also CLOTHING AND ACCESSORIES.)

First of all you need to decide whether to buy or hire and then whether to do so at home or in the resort. If you're a beginner, there is no point in buying skis and boots. Once you have the bug and have reached intermediate standard, you might consider getting your own gear.

If you hire in Britain, you'll get the chance to try the boots on a dry slope (or at least wear them round the house), and if they hurt or are loose, change them. On the other hand, you will be burdened with extra baggage. You can hire from Airport Skis (Gatwick and Manchester) who will reimburse you if the boots don't fit and you have to re-hire in the resort.

Hiring in the resort could waste a lot of time. Everyone in your package tour group will probably rush to the hire shop on the first morning, the staff may be overworked, communication might be tricky and you could be ill-fitted. If not totally satisfied with your equipment, take it back and change it. Painful boots and unsuitable skis can ruin a holiday.

Boots should fit snugly and the heel should not lift up when leaning forward. Don't do them up too tightly (it will cut the circulation and be very painful), nor pad out boots that are too big with several layers of socks. Rear-entry boots are easiest to deal with for a beginner. Classic clip boots give more control to expert skiers.

Your forearm should be parallel with flat ground when holding the pole. To test this, turn the pole upside down and grip it below the basket. You can either choose a pole with a sword grip (easy to use) or strap (less likely to get lost in a fall). Most poles have a combination of both.

Opinions on the right length of ski follow fashion trends. Much depends on the type of ski (e.g. recreational, special, competition), and the weight and ability of the skier. If you get a ski which is either too long or too stiff it will spoil your skiing. Beginners should go for flexible, relatively short skis

for easy turning. Stiff, long skis require precision technique, **E**
but will hold icy slopes better. Flexible skis, however,
perform best in powder snow.

Buyers and hirers alike should ensure that the shop
technician has regulated the binding (DIN) setting to suit the
weight and ability of the skier.

Finally, look after your skis. Get them hot-waxed every
two days (even hire skis) for optimum performance. Keep
the edges sharp to maintain control on hard-packed snow.
Save money by learning how to do it yourself.

GETTING THERE. (See also BOOKING.) **G**

Air. If booking independently, you need to decide whether
to travel by scheduled or charter flight. Tour operators often
offer charter-flight seats at lower fares than those on
scheduled services. However, scheduled services are also
discounted through flight sales agencies close to the date of
departure. These agencies advertise in national newspapers
and are often good for last-minute bargains. Normally,
though, there is a bewildering array of tickets for scheduled
services, with prices for the same class of seating varying
greatly depending on when you book and how long you want
to stay.

If you are travelling on a tour operator's charter flight,
there may well also be space on their connecting coach, so
buying a seat right through to the resort would save you
trouble. Otherwise, in Italy, the public buses to resorts leave
from the city centre, so you will need to catch the regular
service from the airport to the city terminal.

Coach. Italy is particularly far off by land, and coach travel
all the way is seldom an enjoyable experience. However,
north-western Italy is much closer than the north-central or
Dolomite (north-eastern) ski areas. There is a regular coach
service from London Victoria coach station to Milan via the
Aosta Valley and Turin. For details of this and other services,
phone (01) 730 0202.

Rail. Most people prefer rail travel to coach, as it is faster and
more comfortable. When the Channel Tunnel opens, jour-
neys to the nearer Alpine resorts may well be quicker by

G train, if you consider the time spent getting to airports and checking in on top of the flight time, not to mention an often lengthy transfer by coach from the arrival airport to the resort. Much of Italy's skiing, however, is still a long way by train. The Dolomites are passed to the west by the Brenner Pass railways, running from Innsbruck down through Bolzano, and there is a branch line at Fortezza which goes along the north of the area, but it is normally a 50/100-km. journey to your resort from the nearest railway station. There are also a number of "Ski Express" services running from Holland and Germany along this route.

North-central Italy is much the same, the exception being the Aosta Valley, which is reached easily from France via the Fréjus rail tunnel. First stop in Italy is Bardonecchia, the second is Oulx, from where resorts on the Milky Way are accessible (Cesana, Claviere, Sansicario, Sauze d'Oulx, Sestriere). Further down the valley, Courmayeur, La Thuile and others are reasonably accessible from this rail route, which goes on to Turin.

Combining driving and rail travel is possible, though rather expensive, unless the cost is divided among four passengers. The French Motorail system is particularly efficient. There are car-train services from Paris (Bercy) to Milan, Boulogne to Milan, Brussels to Milan and Düsseldorf to Bolzano.

If travelling with skis, you are advised to register these three to four days before departure at the registered baggage office at Victoria Station. You will need to take your ticket along with you.

For information on rail travel in Europe, contact the European Rail Travel Centres to be found at major railway stations in most British cities. They can help you with fares, timetables and bookings.

Cross-Channel Ferry. There are plenty of ferry crossings each day. Remember sea conditions tend to be rougher in winter. A trip by Hovercraft is quicker and only slightly more expensive, but crossings are occasionally cancelled due to high seas. Some ferry lines offer special ski-package rates.

The longer crossing (six hours in the daytime or eight hours overnight) from Harwich to the Hook of Holland is worth considering, and apart from cabin accommodation, costs very little more than the shorter cross-Channel routes. This puts you in the best position to connect with the EuroCity express trains that run down through Germany to the Dolomites.

HEALTH AND MEDICAL CARE

Even minor skiing injuries can turn out to be very expensive to treat, and a major accident could ruin you if your medical insurance were not adequate (see INSURANCE). Citizens of fellow EEC states are entitled to claim the same public health services as those available to resident Italians. Britons should obtain the relevant E111 form from their local office of the Department of Health and Social Security before departure.

Italian doctors should not normally ask for cash on the spot. Make sure you get official receipts for everything: rescue service, doctor's or hospital fees, chemist prescriptions. Put in a claim as soon as you get home. There's usually a deadline.

If you are in need of medical care, it is best to ask your tour representative or hotel receptionist to help you find a doctor (or dentist) who speaks English. Local health units of the Italian National Health Service are listed in the telephone directory under "Unità Sanitaria Locale". The first-aid (pronto soccorso) section of municipal hospitals handle medical emergencies.

Mountain weather is deceptive (see CLIMATE), and not taking the correct precautions or being adequately dressed (see CLOTHING AND ACCESSORIES) can have serious repercussions. Here are a few of the hazards and what to do if the worst happens:

Altitude sickness. Altitude alone affects many people. Mild altitude sickness experienced at around 3,000 m. includes severe headache, nausea and dizziness, but symptoms retreat within an hour of returning to base (your family doctor can prescribe a medicament to prevent this).

H **Sunburn.** Even on a cloudy day you can burn. Put plenty of high protection cream (Factor 15) on exposed areas, concentrating on nose, lips, ears. Apply half an hour before going out to enable the skin to absorb it and reapply often.

Snowblindness occurs when the eyes are not adequately protected. The thin air at high altitude and reflection of the sun off the snow damages the eyes. The result can be most uncomfortable, somewhat like having sand or grit under the eyelids. Stay in a darkened room and bathe the eyes with a soothing lotion. Normal sight will return, but the cornea may suffer permanent damage.

Frostbite is when body tissue actually freezes. First signs are white patches on the face (especially nose and ears) and extremities and a total loss of sensation, even of cold. Usually, if the frostbite is on an exposed part of the body, it is a companion who first notices. If it is not too far advanced, a warm hand over the affected area or rewarming numb and icy fingers under the armpits will be sufficient to bring back sensation. *Never* rub a frostbitten part with snow. More advanced frostbite leads to blistering and a greyish-blue colouring of the area. These are very serious symptoms and immediate expert medical treatment is vital.

Hypothermia is the dangerous lowering of the body temperature. Symptoms are somnolence, apathy and lack of coordination, gradually leading to loss of consciousness. It is particularly common in avalanche victims, but can also be the result of insufficient nourishment, combined with extreme cold, high winds or wet. Again, it is the quick reaction of a companion that can avert more dangerous consequences. Get the victim warm, by putting on extra clothing or a covering—a hat, windjackets, sleeping bags or space blankets—that shield from the wind and conserve body heat. Huddling together or sharing body warmth can also be effective. If the victim is fully conscious, administer warm drinks. *Don't* give alcohol, it accelerates loss of body heat; and *don't* encourage the victim to move around to get warm.

Injury on the mountain. Place crossed skis about 15 m. **H** above the victim and ensure he is as warm and as comfortable as possible. Send a good skier to the nearest lift station: the attendant will radio the piste patrol, who are qualified to assess and deal with the injuries and transport the casualty to the doctors or ambulance. They will also decide whether a helicopter rescue is necessary. Keep in mind that the piste patrol is not necessarily responsible for the safety and rescue of off-piste skiers (see SNOW CONDITIONS).

The international distress signal in the mountains is six shouts or whistles a minute, followed by a minute's silence. Three calls or whistles a minute with a minute's silence is the reply.

HOLIDAYS

Resorts in Italy are busy over Christmas and the New Year and, if the snow is still good, at Easter. Italian children have no February half-term holiday as in many other European countries, but it is traditional for families to head for the mountains over carnival week in February, the exact dates varying from year to year depending on when Easter has been set.

INSURANCE (See also BOOKING and HEALTH AND MEDICAL **I** CARE.)

Many tour operators insist that you take their insurance (partly to ensure you are adequately covered), so check it out well and if necessary take out additional coverage independently. Never economize on insurance.

Ideally, your travel insurance will cover you fully for the following eventualities:

- cancellation or curtailment
- loss or theft of baggage en route, belongings in the resort
- loss or theft of personal money
- breakage of equipment
- illness
- accident on or off the slopes
- rescue service

  - third party or personal liability, i.e., damage done by you
    to someone else or to their property

Useful benefits not covered by all policies:

- missed departure, due to car accident or breakdown, or
  failure of public transport to deliver you to your departure
  airport on time (provided you have left sufficient time)
- facility for a friend or relative to stay on in the resort with
  you if you can't travel immediately or, if necessary, travel
  with you on a different flight from the rest of the package
  tour group
- loss of earnings due to the effects of an injury resulting from
  your ski accident
- refund on lift pass for every ski day lost through injury

Look closely at the exclusion clauses which state the
circumstances in which an insurance company won't settle a
claim. On each claim, there is usually an "excess", which is
the difference between what the insurance company will pay
out and the amount the claimant actually lost or paid. The
amount varies from policy to policy.

L LIFTS

New and more efficient lift systems are being introduced all
the time as more and more skiers want to get up the mountain
faster than ever. The trend is now to replace inefficient old
lifts rather than build lifts into new areas. Italy tends to
have more button-style lifts than other European skiing
nations, but these are generally the more modern lightweight variety. Cable cars are not so common, but this, of
course, does depend on the resort.

Drag and tow lifts. These pull you up the mountain on your
skis. One type consists of a saucer-sized disc or "button"
which you slip between your legs and place behind your
bottom. First-timers should remember *not* to sit down, to
keep their skis parallel and to relax as much as possible. If
you sit down, the elastic wire will give way under your
weight and you will fall over. Your first time on a drag lift is an

unnerving experience, but most lift operators are sympa- **L**
thetic and will slow the lift down and help you on if you
manage to communicate your fears to them.

It is fair to say that T-bars, which pull up two people at a
time, are universally unpopular. It helps to pick a partner the
same size. Tips for riding them well include leaning inwards
and keeping the outer ski slightly forwards.

Chair lifts have improved in leaps and bounds over the
years, going from single chairs right up to four-seater
express lifts which slow down to let you on, then accelerate
off at breakneck speed. Advantages: you don't need to take
off your skis, so they are quick and easy, and it's pleasant to
sit and relax on a sunny day. They are also a good way down
from the higher slopes if the low ones are balding or difficult
to ski for other reasons. Disadvantages: it can be freezing on
a chair lift (some have built-in covers to wrap around you as
you ascend); if it's windy they close them down, but on the
odd occasion when you're going up on one just before the
wind is considered too strong to operate it, the ride can be
most uncomfortable; they have a habit of stopping and
bouncing mid-route.

Télécabines (often called "eggs" or "bubbles") are little
cabins varying from two- to eight-seater expresses, which
you sit in, placing skis in a rack outside. They take you way
up the mountain in some comfort and you are protected from
the elements. They, too, can be closed in strong winds.

Cable cars have reached mammoth proportions over the
years. You stand in them, holding your skis. They can carry
over 150 skiers at a time. Every new one installed takes a few
extra skiers, so the resort can boast the biggest cable car, for
a while.

Lift passes. Choosing the right type of lift ticket to suit your
needs can be difficult. This is especially the case in Italy
where different resorts do not seem keen to work together to
provide more useful combinations for the skier. In some
resorts in Italy, you may have to choose between different
passes within the resort itself, as sets of lifts are operated by

L individual companies. There are notable exceptions: the "Dolomiti-Superski" pass, which for over 20 years has represented the world's largest ski area on one pass—450 lifts, 1,050 km. of piste and 38 ski centres, to be exact.

But generally speaking, if you're a beginner, there is no need to get a pass for the whole area. In fact, in many resorts you may not need a lift at all for the first day or two, so you should find out whether you can get a pass for a shorter period. In many cases, a special beginner's lift pass/equipment/tuition package represents the best value and best sense. Another option is the punch card. You purchase a card with so many points and each lift is worth a certain number which the operator punches off the card before you ascend.

More advanced skiers can either buy an expensive daily lift pass or a pass for any period from two days to a season (six days for a week's holiday by air, 13 for two weeks). For the interlinking ski areas, there is sometimes the option to buy a pass covering them all, though in Italy this is rare. Usually it is a matter of buying a daily extension.

Don't forget to ask for a piste map when you get your ticket. And bring a passport-sized photo with you from home to stick on your pass.

Easy runs are marked green; blue are slightly more tricky; red increasingly so. Blacks are for the foolhardy intermediates to attempt, advanced skiers to try and experts to come down looking good. Icy conditions, slushy melting snow, fog or a blizzard naturally make the runs more difficult to ski.

M MONEY MATTERS

Currency. The *lira* (plural: *lire*; abbreviated *L,* or *Lit.*). Coins come in denominations of L. 5, 10, 20, 50, 100, 200 and 500. Notes: L. 1,000, 2,000, 5,000, 10,000, 50,000 and 100,000.

Credit cards and traveller's cheques. Major credit cards and traveller's cheques are accepted in many Italian shops, restaurants and hotels, but not at petrol stations. But, you will get better value if you change your traveller's cheques at a bank or *cambio*. Eurocheques are easily cashed in Italy.

Banks and currency-exchange offices. Banking hours are
normally from Monday to Friday, 8.30 a.m. to 1.30 p.m. and
sometimes again from 3 to 4 p.m., but this varies from branch
to branch. For security reasons, many banks require
customers to deposit their baggage in a locker prior to
entering, after which you pass through double doors into the
bank itself. Currency-exchange bureaus can be found at
major railway stations, airports and hotels. These are
generally open on weekends and holidays, as well as during
normal working hours. Remember to take your passport
along when cashing traveller's cheques.

PRICES

Prices in Italian ski resorts vary according to the altitude,
how fashionable the resort is, and whether someone owns a
monopoly of, say, the discotheques. Though people talk
about Austria and Switzerland as expensive countries, the
prices in bars and restaurants are really very similar across
the Alps. It seems that, wherever you are, once you go above
1,000 m., the price goes up too.

Even within a resort, prices will differ considerably. A
pizza may cost you more than you will pay in your home
country, but it will be the real thing. Nightlife is invariably
expensive, unless you find a nice hotel discotheque—often
more fun than the "official" ones. If an entrance fee is
charged, check whether it includes a drink. Otherwise be
prepared to pay some incredible prices. Soft drinks do not
necessarily cost less than alcoholic ones. Some resorts have
"snow bars" on their ski runs, where enterprising locals
compete for custom, and prices are much more reasonable.

Remote Livigno up by the Swiss border is duty free, and
supermarket prices for cigarettes, alcoholic drinks and
perfume are far less than what you would pay for similar
articles at airports or on board ferries.

The following prices will give you a rough idea in local
currency of what to expect, but with inflation ever-present,
they should only be regarded as approximate:

P **Airport transfer.** *Milan*: Bus from Linate to city centre L. 2,500; taxi L. 25,000–30,000.

Entertainment. Cinema L. 5,000–9,000. Admission to discotheque L. 5,000, including drink L. 8,000.

Equipment hire. *Skis:* adults L. 13,000–18,000 per day, children L. 8,500–11,000 per day; *boots:* adults L. 5,000–7,000 per day, children L. 4,500–6,500 per day.

Cigarettes (packet of 20). Italian brands L. 1,600 and up, foreign brands L. 2,500–3,000.

Hotels (double room). ***** from L. 200,000, **** from L. 110,000, *** from L. 70,000, ** from L. 45,000, * from L. 40,000.

Kindergarten. Average L. 200,000 for six full days, including lunch.

Meals and drinks. Continental breakfast, mountain lunch, set menu from L. 7,000, lunch/dinner in fairly good establishment L. 17,000–50,000, beer/soft drink L. 1,500–2,000, bottle of wine (in restaurant) L. 9,500.

Supermarket. Milk, per litre L. 1,100; bread per kg. L. 1,800; coffee 100 g. L. 800; butter 100 g. L. 800.

S SKI SCHOOLS

The Italian Ski School *(Scuola Nazionale Italiana di Sci)* is recognized by its distinctive and colourful snowflake logo.

Generally speaking you will be taught the traditional method of learning through snowploughs progressing to parallel turns. After that there is usually some specialist tuition available in race skiing or, in some resorts, monoskiing, surf ("snurf") skiing and perhaps even ski hanggliding or para-skiing.

You can either go into group lessons or take a private instructor. If you choose to go in a group make sure it is of the right standard. Often in Italy there is a test for those who are not complete beginners to establish their level—a short, shallow descent with perhaps one or two turns. The instructors will then allot you a class. If you feel that you are in either a too slow or too advanced group, it is usually easy to move up or down, though it is best to check that your instructor agrees.

There can be up to six different ability levels in a normal **S**
Italian ski school. Try to get an instructor who speaks English,
for obvious reasons, though it is not essential, as body
language can usually indicate what's required and what you
are doing wrong (or right!). Most groups have around seven
or eight members. If there are more than that, you are likely
to find yourself waiting around for each person to do their
bit. Lessons are normally for two hours in the morning or
afternoon.

Private tuition is available by the hour, half day, full day or
even by the week. It costs considerably more, but you do
learn faster.

Some tour operators have "ski guides" in the resorts (and
very occasionally ski instructors). Ski guides should not be
confused with ski instructors, as for one thing it upsets the
local ski school very much. Guides are sometimes qualified
ski instructors, but they cannot call themselves such, and
their main purpose is to show intermediate or advanced
skiers on holiday with a particular tour operator around the
area. It's usually a free service.

SNOW CONDITIONS (See also CLIMATE.)

As already mentioned, early season (December) is a
gamble, except in Sestriere where there's snow-making, or
resorts with high altitude year-round glacier skiing such as
Cervinia. Otherwise there has been a lack of snow in recent
years at this time of year. Snow in January is usually crisp, dry
and a dream to ski. But it can be bitterly cold. Again not a
good choice for a novice. In January and February, lower
resorts—and these are often the prettier, traditional ones
with more atmosphere are usually snow-sure. February is
best if it weren't for school holidays (see HOLIDAYS) in many
European countries, when families head for the Alps. March
is warmer, sunnier and altogether more pleasant. However,
it can get patchy on the runs leading down to the village, and
sunshine, combined with fewer snowfalls and overnight
freezing, results in some icy starts. This is not always the
case: metres of powder snow can fall in spring. April is more
risky and you should select a high altitude resort for best
conditions.

S   Pistes are generally hard-packed as they are bashed down by skiers or special machines as soon as the fresh snow falls. Off piste refers to areas that are not bashed by machines or skied regularly. You shouldn't leap into this great white wilderness unless you're an expert. Even then, you should make sure you know the mountain, otherwise you can never tell what may be lurking under the snow or round the next bend. If you are at all unfamiliar with the terrain, take an instructor or guide. In particular, take special notice of avalanche warnings (yellow and black checked flag). Don't go off piste on a glacier; there is a danger of crevasses, large cracks in the ice sometimes concealed by snow. Remember that if anything should go wrong, patrols are irregular or non-existent away from the pistes. Snow and the mountains may appear innocuous, but they claim many lives every year.

You'll find different types of snow on or off piste. If you thought it was simply white flakes falling out of the sky, you'll discover differently when skiing.

Powder snow. The proverbial skier's dream: crystals of light, dry snow that cannot be formed into a ball. Off piste you float through it; freshly packed down on piste it is easy to glide over. Not all fresh snow is powder: if the weather is warmer, big, wet flakes will fall and that's not the same thing at all. Always beware of avalanches off piste after a heavy snowfall.

Hardpack. This common piste condition results from snow which has been compressed over a few days without a snowfall. Moguls (bumps) form, and icy or even bare patches develop should it not snow again for a while.

Porridge is snow which has been chopped up by skiers. It can refer to fresh snow which has been skied over without being bashed by the piste machines. Or in spring when it is warmer and the sun shines, surface snow softens and the pistes get slushy.

Spring snow (also known as corn snow) is lovely to ski, especially off piste. Smooth, wet snow freezes overnight, and first thing in the morning the texture is like granulated sugar. When the surface has just softened, it develops a sheen. This snow is very easy to ski but sadly short-lived. By lunchtime it has generally become slushy, but is good to monoski in. **Windslab** is an off-piste condition caused by wind blowing powder snow and depositing it in the lee of the mountain, packing it down hard and seemingly unbreakable. It is very dangerous, as great chunks break away in slab avalanches. **Breakable crust.** This happens to fresh snow off piste when the surface melts during the day and freezes overnight. It is very difficult to ski over.

TELEPHONE

Gettoni, tokens valid at L. 200, are available from post offices, tobacconists, bars and news-stands. You need about 30 for a three-minute call to northern Europe, which means more or less that you have to insert one coin every six seconds. Telephones also accept L. 100 and 200 coins. You can insert more than one at a time and unused coins are returned. International calls can be made from boxes marked ''Teleselezione''.

Some public phones can be used with cards valid at L. 6,000 and 9,000, but these are still rare. Where they do exist, cards may be purchased from SIP (Italian Telephone Service) offices.

The dialling tone is normally a series of long dash sounds. A dot dot dot series means the central computer is overloaded, so hang up and try again.

International calls are best made from hotels (usually at a surcharge) or special agencies. Or else you can book a call at the local public telephone office *(Posto Telefonico Pubblico)*.

TOURIST INFORMATION OFFICES

The Italian State Tourist Office *(Ente Nazionale Italiano per il Turismo,* abbreviated ENIT) is represented in Italy and abroad. For the UK, the office is at 1, Princes Street, London W1R 8AY, tel. (01) 408 1254.

Each resort will also have a local tourist office which can supply brochures and piste maps and answer queries.

Information is also available from the Federazione Italiana Sport Invernali, 44B, Via Piranesi, Milan, tel. (02) 719 751.

SOME USEFUL EXPRESSIONS

Equipment

I'd like to hire/buy ...	Vorrei noleggiare/comprare
ski boots	degli scarponi da sci
ski poles	dei bastoncini da sci
skis	degli sci
What length poles/ skis should I have?	Per me di che lunghezza devono essere i bastoncini/ gli sci?
Can you adjust the bindings?	Può regolare gli attacchi?
Can you wax my skis?	Può dare la sciolina ai miei sci?
Can you sharpen the edges?	Può affilare le lamine?
I am a ...	Sono un/una ...
beginner	principiante
intermediate skier	sciatore medio/sciatrice media
advanced skier	buon sciatore/buona sciatrice
I weigh ... kilos.	Peso ... chili.
My shoe size is ...	Il mio numero di scarpe è il ...

British	4	5	6	6½	7	8	8½	9	9½	10	11
Continental	37	38	39	40	41	42	43	43	44	44	45

These boots are ...	Questi scarponi sono ...
too big/too small	troppo grandi/troppo piccoli
uncomfortable	scomodi
Do you have any rear-entry boots?	Hai scarponi con apertura posteriore?

Problems

My skis are too long/ too short.	I miei sci sono troppo lunghi/ troppo corti.
My ski/pole has broken.	Si è rotto uno sci/un bastoncino.
My bindings are too loose/too tight.	Gli attacchi sono troppo allentati/troppo stretti.

218

The clasp on my boot is broken.	Si è rotto il gancio del mio scarpone.
My boots hurt me.	Gli scarponi mi fanno male ai piedi.

Clothing and accessories

bumbag	il marsupio
gloves	i guanti
goggles	gli occhiali da neve
hat	la cuffia
headband	la fascia per capelli
jacket	la giacca
mittens	le manopole
one-piece suit	una tuta intera
polo-neck sweater	un maglione dolcevita
rucksack	uno zaino
ski suit	un completo da sci
ski trousers	i pantaloni da sci
socks	le calze
sun glasses	gli occhiali da sole

and don't forget:

lip salve	la pomata per le labbra
sun cream	la crema solare

Lifts and lift passes

I'd like a ...	Vorrei ...
lift pass	un abbonamento
day	giornaliero
season	stagionale
week	settimanale
I'd like a book of ... lift coupons.	Vorrei un blocchetto di ... abbonamenti a punti.
ten/twenty/thirty	dieci/venti/trenta
Do I need a photo?	Occorre una fotografia?
Could I have a lift-pass holder?	Potrei avere una busta plastica per l'abbonamento
cable car	funivia
chair lift	seggiovia
drag lift	sciovia

gondola	telecabina
Where's the end of the queue?	Dov'è la fine della coda?
Can I have a piste map, please?	Potrei avere una carta delle piste

On the piste

Where are the nursery slopes?	Dove sono le piste per principianti?
Which is the easiest way down?	Qual è la pista più facile?
It's a(n) ... run.	È una pista ...
easy/difficult	facile/difficile
gentle/steep	in leggera pendenza/ ripida
green (very easy)	verde (molto facile)
blue (easy)	blu (facile)
red (intermediate)	rossa (media)
black (difficult)	nera (difficile)
The piste is closed.	La pista è chiusa.
The piste is very icy.	La pista è molto ghiacciata.
... snow	neve...
deep	alta
powder	farinosa
sticky	appiccicosa
mogul (bump)	la gobba
rock	la roccia
tree	l'albero
Watch out!	Attenzione!

Ski school

I'd like some skiing lessons.	Vorrei prendere lezioni di sci.
group/private	in gruppo/private
Is there an English-speaking instructor?	C'è un maestro che parli in glese?

If the answer's no, then the following will come in handy:

snowplough	la spazzaneve
stem christie	la cristiania
parallel turn	la curva parallela

downhill ski	sci a valle
uphill ski	sci a monte
Weight on the downhill ski.	Peso sullo sci a valle.
Bend your knees.	Piegate le ginocchie.
Tuck your bottom in.	In avanti il sedere.
You're sitting too far back.	State tenendo il sedere troppo indietro.
Lean forward.	Piegatevi in avanti.
Traverse the piste ...	Attraversate la pista ...
slowly	lentamente
faster	più forte
Slow down.	Rallentate.
Stop.	Fermatevi.
Follow me.	Seguitemi.
Shoulders towards the valley.	Spalle a valle
Up-down-up.	Su-giù-su.
Unweight your skis.	Scaricate i vostri sci.
Transfer your weight now.	Spostate il vostro peso di lato.
left/right	sinistro/destro
herring bone	a spina di pesce
side-stepping	il passo a scala
side-slipping	lo slittamento
Poles behind you.	Bastoncini indietro.
Edge/Flatten your skis.	Spigolate/Appiattite gli sci.
Keep your skis parallel.	Tenete gli sci paralleli.
Put your skis together.	Tenete uniti gli sci.
Keep the skis flat and evenly weighted.	Tenete gli sci piatti e ripartite il peso equamente.

Emergencies

I can't move my ...	Non posso muovere ...
My ... hurts.	Mi fa male ...
back	la schiena
finger	il dito
knee	il ginocchio
neck	il collo
wrist	il polso

I've pulled a muscle.	Ho un strappo muscolare.
Please get help.	Per favore, cercate aiuto.
Don't move.	Non muovetevi.
avalanche danger	pericolo di valanghe
rescue service	il servizio soccorso

Relaxing

massage	il massaggio
sauna	la sauna
skates	i pattini
skating rink	la pista di pattinaggio
swimming pool	la piscina
beer	la birra
cake	la torta
chips	le patatine fritte
coffee	il caffè
dish of the day	il piatto del giorno
pastry	i pasticcini
(mountain) restaurant	il ristorante (di montagna)
salad	l'insalata
sandwich	il panino imbottito
sausage	la salsiccia
tea	il tè
(mulled) wine	il vino brûlé

INDEX

An asterisk (*) after a page number indicates a map reference. Where there is more than one set of page references, the one in bold type refers to the main entry. For index to Practical Information, see p. 193.